How To Become Head Of Your Firm Before Forty

How To Become Head Of Your Firm Before Forty

by

JOHN D. HORN

COLERIDGE PRESS

NEW YORK

HOW TO BECOME HEAD OF YOUR FIRM BEFORE FORTY
COPYRIGHT © 1964 BY JOHN D. HORN

LIBRARY OF CONGRESS CATALOG NUMBER: 63-22043

PRINTED IN THE UNITED STATES OF AMERICA

**To My Wife
Daisy**

FOREWORD

Would you like to become president of your firm before you're forty?

Ask that question, offhand, to the average young man (and many young women) employed in commerce today, and most of the time you'll get this quick answer: "Sure I would." (I know that's the answer you would get because it *is* the answer I have gotten most of the times I've asked that question.)

But would these young people really like to be at the head of their firms? Of course, they would like to have the money and prestige that goes with the top job in an American corporation. However, most of the very same people, if confronted with the sacrifices which a company president must make day in and day out, would soon realize that they are not cut out to guide a firm which has tremendous responsibilities to employees, stockholders and the public alike.

That question, and the answers I got whenever I asked it, began to intrigue me soon after I became president of my firm, in 1958. I was then 32, and had been with my company nine years. The more logical thought I applied to this matter, and the more I discussed it with others, the more I was intrigued. A year ago I determined to spend some off-the-job time taking a hard-headed, businesslike look at the subject.

I talked with corporation presidents, and people on their way to becoming corporation presidents. I talked with these people at conventions, across the lunch table, on trains and planes all across the country. I wrote to scores of others. I went to the public library and read what I could find that had been written by corporation presidents, present and past, on getting ahead in business.

When I began this investigation, I was just curious. Becoming head of a corporation before forty was nothing unique, I knew. Hundreds and hundreds of American business men had done it — and they're doing it all the time, more and more. But, as I learned more and more about these men who had become corporation heads, many of them at comparatively early ages, a pattern seemed to be emerging.

I wondered if there were a formula. Was it *chance* or was it *planning* that put these young men at the head of big firms? Was it *luck* or was it *hard work?* Was it *personality* or was it *perseverance?* The further I pursued this study, the more it appeared that it is all these qualities — and more — that account for rapid rises to the top in American business.

Then came the suggestion: "What you are learning here should be helpful to a lot of young people wanting to climb to the top in business. Why not set down your findings? Why not dress up your conclusions a bit and wrap up the whole thing in a book? Maybe somebody would find it useful. Maybe it would help some promising young businessman get to the top quicker. Maybe it would help young people avoid some of the mistakes that kept you out of the president's chair till you were well past thirty."

I was challenged. Result: this book. I hope it will help *you.* I shall be grateful to hear if, and how, it does.

J. D. H.

CONTENTS

How To Become Head Of Your Firm Before Forty

1

BE SURE OF YOUR GOAL

If you are to become head of your firm, ever . . . there is one thing before all others that you must possess.

If you are to become head of your firm before you are forty years old, you must possess and command this most valuable asset as soon as possible.

You may have one of the most brilliant minds ever known in the business world . . . but, if you do not possess this vital inner quality, you'll never make it to the top.

Lady Luck may be at your side, every minute of every day . . . but, without this all-important resource, you're sure to be stopped short of the top.

You may work hard, night and day, like a hive of honeybees in Spring, but all your effort won't put you in that chair marked "President" unless you have this *first ingredient*, this most essential element, this *sine qua non* to success.

Call it AMBITION. . . call it DESIRE . . . call it ASPIRATION, YEARNING, PURPOSE, DETERMINATION, RESOLVE . . . even call it PASSION . . . call it what you will — *unless you really want to become head of your firm, there's no use trying.*

How Can You Be Sure?

If you're the only son in a family that owns a corporation, perhaps your mind has already been made up for you. . . ever since you were born. Maybe your wife's family owns a corporation. It has happened that way for some company presidents. Some wag once said there are four main ways of getting to where you'll have to worry about money (from having so much) :

3

    (1) select rich parents;

    (2) marry a rich girl;

    (3) hit the long shots every time you bet;

or, (4) work hard.

Of course, we must recognize all those *possible* avenues to financial good fortune and the sort of good life we all respect as worthy to be sought after. But, both observation and experience tell most of us that we shall have to pursue those meritorious objectives by other avenues — missing all those ways except the fourth. Yes, *hard work* is perhaps the main road you'll take on your way to becoming head of your firm, but it's not the only one. (*Hard work* heads the list of "major factors" to which a group of outstanding corporation presidents attributed their own successful climbs up the executive ladder, in a survey I made in preparing this book . . . but more about that later.)

Should You Try?

Not everyone should even try to reach for the top. Many would be unhappy there. Others would lack the motivation and many would perhaps lack the stamina to stay on top, even if they were to succeed in reaching it.

I know of a young man of great intellectual ability who really wanted to be a research scientist, but his wife pushed him into striving for higher and higher executive jobs. She wanted the prestige that goes with being the wife of a high-level executive. He made rapid strides up the executive ladder, because of his exceptional intelligence and because he was spurred on by his wife. Before he reached the top, however, he developed ulcers. A few months of treatment by a psychiatrist revealed his incompatibility with the role he was playing, Both he and his wife did much soul-searching. He decided to quit his job. He went to work in a small research laboratory. Now he's happy. What's more, his wife has found that she has just as much prestige as the wife of a brilliant young research scientist as she would if he were president of his old firm.

Why Do YOU Work?

If you want to avoid such time-wasting mistakes as that young executive was driven into, you'll make sure of a few things about yourself before you get on that executive ladder leading to the top of your firm. You'll do some soul-searching, and some hard-headed self-analysis. You'll subject yourself to whatever valid tests you can find — to satisfy yourself that you are "presidential timber."

One of the most trustworthy tests of whether or not you are actually capable of developing into the head of your firm (whether you are a potential president) is to honestly ask yourself:

Do I enjoy my work for itself?
(Or, am I working to achieve something
entirely different?)

Be honest with yourself — brutally honest. Don't answer that question too quickly. If you can't answer that italicized question with a loud, firm "Yes" . . . well, maybe you'd better settle for a vice-presidency as your goal.

You know of businessmen, I am sure, who have accumulated enough money and prestige to last any man for a lifetime, yet they still work just as hard as ever. Many business heads are in that category — most of the outstanding ones, I believe.

"Why doesn't he slow down?" you'll hear somebody ask about such a man. Truth is, he couldn't slow down even if he wanted to. Something inside such a man is burning for expression. Maybe he didn't put it there . . . many will say he was born with it, it's a "gift." Anyway, it's there . . . and it's burning. That man really *enjoys* working. His job is not a chore; it's a means of expression, or fulfillment, or unfoldment. Without his work, that man wouldn't feel he was really living.

Perhaps he has a thousand ideas of products, some of which he feels certain will find places for themselves among consumer preferences. Quite possibly he dreams of merging several corporations in allied fields, to achieve greater economies and thereby benefit both his workers and his customers.

Here is a man to whom money means very little except to realize his dreams. To him, money is a tool, not the goal. He is working because he enjoys the work itself; not because it will bring him fame or fortune, but because he is completely intoxicated by the joy and satisfaction that comes from striving for personal achievement.

If you enjoy your work like that man enjoys his, there's a good chance you're the kind of person who can make the grade.

But that is not the only test.

Presidency Is No Steppingstone

A mistake frequently made by young people just out of school is — using business as a steppingstone to another career objective. One such individual had a phenomenal success in business, but his real goal was to become an ambassador. He reasoned that his best chance to attain such a distinction was to become president of one of the nation's larger corporations . . . so many ambassadors have done it that way. With his tremendous flair for the dramatic and a drive that would not permit either himself or his subordinates to rest, he drove on until he became president of his firm. Before he even had a chance to consolidate his position in this job, which carried immense responsibilities, he began to use his newly-won prestige to work his way into the hierarchy of one of the major political parties. Indeed, he was soon made general chairman of the year's largest fund-raising dinner.

This man's plan was working to perfection — one would have been inclined to conclude. Before long, however, there was evidence to the contrary. His grip on the company started slipping; he was spreading himself too thin. Politics was taking too much of his time and attention. Subordinates sensed his desire to use the company, and them, to help him achieve his own personal political aims. They didn't like it.

Profits began dropping . . . and nobody liked that. In a period of two years, half a dozen top executives resigned. All this was too much for the Board of Directors. Our politically-ambitious company president was asked to share the firm's management with another man. When he refused, the Board asked for his resignation.

Sadly deflated, this ex-president tried to win the nomination to a medium-level political job, only to find that he had practically no support from the professional politicians.

By mistakenly trying to use a corporation presidency as a stepping-stone, he fell flat on his face in politics and in business.

Do not conclude that business and politics don't mix. There is an entirely proper connection between politics (civic affairs) and business; this man just didn't connect them properly.

If your goal is to become head of your firm, don't confuse yourself and possibly throw yourself by regarding that goal as merely a steppingstone.

Aim For More Than Money

Don't try for a lofty executive position just to make money. Chances are you'll never reach the top, then — you'll lack the proper motivation.

If you have a skill or profession, or if you possess a high level of business talent, you may be able to build a personal estate — even a fortune — by going into business for yourself. And taxes will not eat up quite so much of your income that way as when all your income is from salary.*

Furthermore, you may find you can earn more as a lower-level executive in a large firm than you could as head of a smaller company. To a man truly bent on absolute corporate leadership, this will mean very little. To a man who puts money first, the smaller salary for a job which obviously demands more time and carries greater responsibility will never make sense. (There you have another excellent test to help you decide whether or not you are psychologically attuned to a job which will demand your very "all" if and when you reach the goal.)

What Are The ESSENTIAL QUALITIES?

But, you no doubt are wondering, what kind of qualities must a man have to qualify as true presidential timber?

The answer is not simple.

I have seen excellent corporation presidents who are so shy they seldom talk unless spoken to. I've seen others as gregarious as the most overbearing high-pressure salesman. Some are tactful; others, tactless. Some are brilliant, while others are little more than high-average in native intelligence. There simply is no personality pattern, visible to the naked eye, which marks one man as a presidential probability while obviously destining another for a place somewhat lower in the corporate structure.

Nevertheless, there are certain signs which you can look for in yourself to help you decide if your goal of attaining a corporation presidency is the right one for you. (These signs have to do, mainly, with character traits — *what you are,* as distinguished from primarily external but nonetheless essential factors — *what you do.*) Surprisingly, perhaps, these (*what-you-are*) signs will be obvious to yourself, but even your closest friend or your wife may not have the slightest idea of how you feel about them.

At the end of this chapter are questions designed to give you an insight into yourself on this one subject. Your answers will cast a little light on your aptitude and personality for the top executive job, but they will in no way indicate whether or not you qualify for a responsible job at some other level short of a corporation presi-

---

* While there are and always will be tremendous opportunities for the man who starts his own business, this volume deals primarily with the much more numerous and less risky opportunities in business firms already established. However, attention is given to establishing new firms in Chapter 28, Another Way To Get To The Top Fast: Start Your Own Business.

dency. Write in your answers to the questions, with coldly objective truthfulness. Remember, it is far better to learn now that you are *not* cut out for corporate leadership than to suffer disappointment and heartbreak later.

"What-You-Do" Factors

A few paragraphs ago I mentioned a difference between *what-you-are* factors and *what-you-do* factors which contribute to advancement in business. I asked a group of outstanding corporation presidents under forty to conscientiously and confidentially list and score the relative importance of major factors in their climbs up the executive ladder. Their answers turned up some interesting, though perhaps not too deeply significant, data on 23 factors contributing to their own successes. You'll find the list at the end of the book (Page 190), in different order than given here. Just for your own interest, before you go on to Chapter 2, rate these factors 1 to 23 in relative importance by *your* considered opinion; then forget your scoring till you finish reading the book. Then, double-check your own scoring (using the column indicated for this), and make any changes you think in order, before comparing your scoreboard with the composite scoreboard of these corporation presidents, on Page 190. I repeat, this may be more interesting than significant. Here is the list:

MAJOR SUCCESS FACTORS

(See results on page 190)

FACTOR	FIRST RATING	CHECK RATING
Ability to make decisions		
Being an expert in something		
Company politics		
Complete knowledge of firm's operation		
Creative thinking		
Delegating responsibility		
Desire to learn		
Detailed career planning		
Enthusiasm for the job and ability to inspire others		
Happy marriage and moral support		
Hard work		
Luck		

MAJOR SUCCESS FACTORS

(*Continued*)

FACTOR	FIRST RATING	CHECK RATING
Opportunism		
Participating in civic affairs		
Planned public relations		
Putting up a front		
Singleness of purpose		
Smooth personal relationships		
Socializing with co-workers		
Socializing with customers		
Tackling tough problems		
Trade association activity		
Monetary incentive		

Easier BEFORE Forty?

This question was put to several score young corporation presidents under forty:

> Do you think it was *harder* or easier for you to become head of your firm *before* 40 than it would have been for you to have moved slower and become president at 50 or 55?

Every respondent replied that it's easier before forty. Among them: *Herman Perl,* one of whose firms in 1959 sold more land than any other real estate outfit in the country. This 37-year-old dynamo went to work at 16. He is either president or chairman of the board of eighteen corporations: real estate, electronics, printing, finance, construction, and so on, with a combined sales force exceeding 1,200.

Jack C. Vaughn, head of Spartan Drilling Company, Dallas, Texas, believes it is easier before forty, "for at a younger age you have more drive and perseverance necessary to get the job done."

James F. Kelly, a North Carolina farm boy who became, at 33, President of Aeroglide Corporation (farm and food machinery), is "inclined to think that the burden of responsibility would be more difficult and a greater strain, emotionally," after forty.

Such opinions are supported by something which the famous British physician, *Sir William Osler,* wrote when he was 70 "Take the sum of human achievement in action, in science, in art, in literature," wrote Sir William, "subtract the work of men above forty, and while we should miss great treasures, even priceless treasures, we would practically be where we are today . . . The effective, moving, vitalizing work of the world is done between the ages of twenty-five and forty."

. . . Words to weigh, and ponder profoundly, as you set your sure goal — to become head of your firm before forty.

QUESTIONS TO INDICATE YOUR APTITUDE AND
PERSONALITY FOR A CORPORATE PRESIDENCY

Mark your answers "Yes" or "No". Then turn to Page 189 for instructions on scoring yourself.

	YES	NO
1. Do you thoroughly enjoy your present job?	___	___
2. Do you regularly spend significantly more time on your job than is required, without feeling that you are doing more than your share?	___	___
3. Are you constantly thinking up ways for your company to make more money, or save money?	___	___
4. Do you frequently feel restless on a weekend and find that the only way you can relax is to sit down and do something constructive about your job or company?	___	___
5. Except for the necessities of your present standard of living, is money relatively unimportant to you?	___	___
6. Do you normally feel slightly uncomfortable when you are in a group and the group does not look to you for leadership or advice?	___	___
7. If you had your choice of attending a social function in a group where you are active or attending a trade association meeting where you will learn something of value to your company, would you choose to attend the trade association meeting?	___	___
8. When you attend a social gathering of close friends, do you prefer to talk about business rather than some other subject?	___	___

YES   NO

9. When you think about your own future career, do you often think about all the constructive things you can do for your company once you receive the authority? ___ ___

10. Do you seldom, if ever, think about the material things you will be able to enjoy when you get the raises you think you will eventually earn? ___ ___

11. Do you have some good ideas, right now, for developing the business of your company to a higher level? ___ ___

12. Do you read the business pages of your newspaper or news magazine because you enjoy it rather than because you feel you need to keep yourself informed on business news? ___ ___

13. Have you ever made a study, on your own, of business trends or some other area of business that was not required in your work? ___ ___

14. Have you, in the past six months, picked up a book on some business subject other than your primary specialization simply because you want to develop a more well-rounded understanding of all business procedures and practices? ___ ___

15. Does it really "hurt" you to see money wasted in your company? ___ ___

16. Do you regularly try to save money for your company when traveling, by flying "coach" or by asking for less than the "best room" in the hotel? ___ ___

17. Do you NEVER worry about someone else making more than you do for a job that carries less responsibility? ___ ___

18. Do you always talk up when a policy is being discussed with which you do not agree, but once the decision is made, support it as if it were your very own idea? ___ ___

YES   NO

19. Do you feel it is far better to try an idea and find out you were wrong than to sit on it and avoid making a mistake? ___ ___

20. Do you try to utilize subordinates to their fullest, developing them and training them in all you know, without any fear that they may make you less needed in the company? ___ ___

21. Is your job more important to you than anything else, except perhaps your family and personal convictions? ___ ___

22. When there is a job to be done that is impossible to accomplish in the normal course of business, do you NEVER say to yourself, "I'll do my best but if that's not enough, I can't help it? ___ ___

23. Do you feel that there is always a way to accomplish the "impossible," by using imagination and making the effort? ___ ___

24. Do you feel your company and you have a great future together? ___ ___

25. Do you often find yourself working long beyond reasonable hours without being even slightly conscious of the time? ___ ___

26. Do you take pride in the accomplishments of your company, even when most of the credit goes to someone other than yourself? ___ ___

27. Do you like to think of your company as a team where every department is going forward toward a common goal? ___ ___

28. Do you enjoy coordinating the activities of people in diversified fields of work? ___ ___

29. Do you feel a burning desire to understand every segment of your company's operations? ___ ___

30. If you were to become president of your company, would you never consider this the realization of your ambitions but rather "just the beginning" for you? ___ ___

2

PICK YOUR COMPANY CAREFULLY

A group of college seniors were discussing aftergraduation plans.

"I wouldn't work for that outfit," said one. "They start you out at only $300 a month."

"I've been considering a job with General Products," said another. "They have a good profit-sharing plan."

"I want to work for a firm that has a program to pay for graduate study," said a third senior, whose big interest was research.

To the man in a banker's-gray suit, with some silver on his temples, these remarks might seem a bit one-sided — especially since these young folk represent tomorrow's business leadership. However, with the high-powered recruiting programs now prevalent among forward-looking business firms, it is understandable why many young people are laying more and more stress on material things . . . why they tend to overlook the longer-range satisfactions which will mean so much more over the forty years or more of their working lives.

Competition for outstanding college graduates is vigorous among firms whose enlightened managements favor early starts in training future executives. If these personnel people fail to make their companies seem more attractive than others, they may see most of the qualified graduates go to more aggressive firms.

But an intelligent and ambitious young person with genuine desire to achieve his own objectives in a businses career will not bite this short-term bait. He will look beyond these glittering lures, or he is in danger of sacrificing his self-satisfaction to a shallow opportunism that may mean disappointment later.

Many Leaders Started At Bottom

In every era, there are some business leaders who start fairly high up the ladder . . . by reason of family wealth, position, marriage, or other factors. Among such persons we might list: Baron Nathan Mayer Rothschild, J. P. Morgan, Winthrop Aldrich, and Richard S. Reynolds, Jr.

But for every person so circumstanced at the beginning of his business career, there are many who have no choice but to start at the bottom. Among such people, who have made big marks in American business, may be mentioned:

Andrew Carnegie, who started at 13 as a weaver's helper in a Pennsylvania cotton mill;

Henry Ford, who started as a machinist-apprentice at 16, and worked for other people until he set up his own business at 40;

John D. Rockefeller, who started as a bookkeeper at 16, and organized his first company at 20;

Walter S. Gifford, who went to work for Western Electric at $10 a week after graduation from Harvard . . . and rose to the top of American Telephone & Telegraph Company;

Frederick H. Ecker, long-time President, then Chairman of the Board, of Metropolitan Life Insurance Company, who "colleged his way through work" rather than working his way through college;

Thomas J. Watson, who started as a salesman for National Cash Register Company, and later guided International Business Machines to its position of world-wide pre-eminence.

A college degree usually helps you start a little higher up the executive ladder. But that is not the big advantage of academic training. Formal schooling equips you, presumably, to think faster, to think better — and thereby climb to the top quicker.

Whether you are in college, in high school, or whether you're now in a fairly good job but feel a bit like a square peg in a round hole . . . this chapter is addressed specifically to you — to help you save time in climbing to the top.

In business careers, as in racing, you sometimes have false starts. Sometimes you "jump the gun" and have to start over again. Sometimes there are other reasons for a bad start. "A good start is half the race," you've heard it said. For most young men and women, a good start in business usually means (primarily) selecting the right employer.

Yes, as a foresighted, ambitious young person with high aims of making your mark in the world of commerce, you should very carefully *pick your employer,* not just wait for some employer, any employer, to pick you.

How Do You Select A Firm
In Which To Build A Satisfying Career?

The problem isn't simple . . . the solution, not too easy. It requires much self-disciplined analysis, as well as courage. You must take a course that's different from that of most other young people.

Among individuals, details will differ, but *here are five basic steps* absolutely vital to making your decision — and it could be the most important decision you'll ever make:

First — Decide Your Career Objective

This first step is always the hardest. Job counselors and placement people in many large American universities tell me that more than half of today's graduates have only a vague idea of what they want to do, long-range. Even after four years of exploring their interests, many college men and women do not make definite career decisions until ready to take a job. Some do not make a final decision until they have held two or three jobs.

This is not necessarily harmful, but you'll save time if you make a sound decision before taking your first real big full-time job.

But, how do you decide?

There's much more to selecting a career objective than simply deciding what general type of work you want to do. Maybe you want to be in marketing. But have you narrowed down your ultimate goal to a particular phase of marketing: advertising, merchandising, purchasing, sales supervision?

Furthermore, if you're now at the point of picking your career company (and/or vice versa), you should know whether your interests lean more toward retailing than toward distribution on a regional or national scale. You should know by now whether you'd prefer to be a storekeeper or a traveling salesman. In other words, now is the time to determine your ultimate goal . . . to define your objective.

(This book was begun with the idea of helping those with the definite goal of a corporation presidency. Maybe your goal is not exactly that, but is in that direction. Then, most of the material herein should be just as useful to you as if you were determined to become a corporation chief executive.)

I know a man who inherited a department store — not one of the biggest, but it gave him an attractive income. It was in an expanding community, so he had opportunity for growth, and there was a measure of personal challenge. He sold the store to take a job as manufacturer's representative — traveling salesman, if you please.

I asked his wife why he gave up a relatively secure future for one of unknown proportions. Her reply was quite revealing:

"Dick always wanted to be part of a larger project. I often saw envy in his eyes when salesmen called on us at the store and told how they introduced new items to some of the larger stores in big cities. I know Dick will be happier now. He simply was not cut out to be a retailer. He's a drummer at heart, and I know he'll be quite successful at selling."

She knew her husband's inclinations and abilities, and she knew the direction in which he should be setting his sights. He was running on the wrong track — for him.

Don't Set Your Sights Too Low

That's another common error in deciding on a career objective.

Modesty is a commendable virtue, sometimes; but if you want to get to the top in any field, you must look and think and work toward the very top, toward absolute leadership. If you are demonstrating enough intelligence to take this problem seriously, there's an excellent chance that you will go much farther in your business career than even you now dream possible.

What are your current assets? What are your aptitudes? Many young people, even after a few years of working, don't have a clear idea of the field in which they would prefer to work. If you're one of these, you may have to go one step farther in setting your objective.

An aptitude test can help you determine the area in which you would be happiest and do your best work. After such a test, you'll be given a list of occupations in which you would be most likely to succeed. Sometimes it's a long list. You'll have to make your own selection.

Your interests, now and up to now, will provide some evidence of the type of work that would give you greatest rewards in personal satisfaction. Take as much time as you need — as much time as you can — to make a sound, definite, firm decision that you can (and will want to) live with the rest of your life.

So, if you have the slightest question about the field where you'll be most satisfied, take that aptitude test. Most colleges will arrange it for you, even though you're not a student. Most large business firms have personnel and facilities for giving such tests. If you're in doubt, take that aptitude test.

But, Why Should You Set A Definite Objective?

Why not take a job in some compatible activitiy, then see where the wind will blow you? A lot of people do just that; but I say to you, Don't! Why?

Because you'll go much farther, faster, by setting your sights on a definite, worthy, and high objective, This will help prevent you from accepting what appears to be an opportunity or an advancement, but which might ultimately lead you down a blind alley, a dead-end job with no room for further growth.

A young friend of mine had a marvelous future in accounting. With a few more years of seasoning, he might have qualified for assistant comptroller and in time might have become treasurer of his firm, a leader in it's field. But he was impatient. He was offered the post of credit manager of a smaller firm, and he accepted — thinking it was a step up the ladder. After ten years, he's still credit manager.

Don't bite the bait he took. In deciding on your career objective, make up your mind you're going to stick with that decision. Then be ready to do like the Chinese do . . . exercise your patience.

Pay is important. Don't overlook that in setting your career objective. Idealistic young people do overlook it, sometimes. Hold on to your idealism . . . but with your eyes and your mind wide open. Remember that a primary purpose of work is to provide for yourself and your family. Salary should not be your only objective, of course; but you'd be foolish to ignore it entirely. Put pay in its proper place, in deciding your objective . . . and give ample thought to this matter as you read and study Chapter 5.

Maybe you're thinking, "I just want to earn as much money as I can."

Don't fool yourself. It's not that simple.

We, as individuals, differ in our desire for, and need for, money — and the things money will buy. Family and other factors often create such a strong need for material benefits that some men are almost forced to give greater importance to income. Others consider money primarily as a means of providing the necessities of life, preferring to give prime importance to other satisfactions.

These are points you can't afford to overlook in your long-range planning. Your decision on a career objective must be within the bounds of the sort of world, the sort of community, you want to live in and work in. If you want to live in a Cadillac community, don't set your sights on a Chevrolet income.

Don't be afraid to examine your conscience on this point, and examine it closely, before you decide on your objective. Don't be afraid to face the facts . . . in your own thinking, your own philosophy, your own innermost desires. Then face those facts cooly, objectively, — but not emotionally.

Take a businesslike, scientific, analytical look at each objective which attracts you. Weigh the *cons* against the *pros*; and if the *pros* do not outweigh the *cons,* then look at another objective.

Finally, in settting your career objective, *be sure the goal you choose is one you are willing and able to work for.*

Some occupations call for more sacrifice than others. You may be required to stay away from your family for weeks at a time. If that's just too much for you or your spouse (or the one who'll someday be your spouse), then pick another objective. Remember, individuals are different. It follows that different objectives and varying levels of achievement are inevitable.

You may select an objective that will never make you famous or wealthy . . . but that's not important if fame and wealth are relatively unimportant in your view. What *is* important is that your career objective be something you genuinely want, something that fits your own philosophy of living. When, after a careful and unbiased appraisal, you've determined the correct answer, the ultimate objective for your business career . . . then you can work toward that goal long and hard, with no fear of drudgery and no fear of ulcers.

Second — Decide Whether Your Objective
Can Best Be Reached In A Small Company Or A Large One

Once your career objective has been set, you are well on your way toward making a satisfactory selection of a career company. A reasoned examination of where you hope to be ten, twenty, or thirty years from now will, of itself, throw a great deal of light on the company you should choose.

As a general rule, the smaller the firm, the less specialized your work will be. You will work on a much broader scope, justifying your salary by specific contributions to the over-all product line.

Thus, generally speaking, you'll have more opportunities for rapid advancement in the smaller company; but when you get to the top you'll probably be making as much as an assistant vice president in a larger firm.

Both small and large companies have their advantages. Again, it's a matter of your personal preference. Only *you* can decide where you will be most successful, and happiest.

Recently a design engineer left his company, one of the largest auto manufacturers. He went with a small industrial designing firm, at a much lower salary. Asked his reason, he said simply: "I was doing a very small part of a big job. Even though it was important, I never felt the satisfaction of complete creation. Now, when I do the entire design job on, say, an electric ironer or a modern ash tray, my wife tells me I glow with pride. When others note the difference, you know I feel it."

Even more significant, in deciding the size of .the career company you choose, is the matter of money. A large firm usually pays a little more at the start, but salary increases are generally smaller than in a medium-size firm.

You'll probably make more the first year or two in a big outfit, but in three or four years you'd probably be earning more with a smaller firm. However, once you reach the top executive level, your salary in a giant corporation will be much greater than with a medium-size corporation.

Similarly, you will probably make more in a smaller firm when you reach the junior executive level, but your financial growth from there on may be limited (compared with opportunities in the big corporations); although you should be able to reach a top-level job faster with a smaller company.

Suppose you want to reach a level equivalent to sales manager, so you can direct marketing policies on a national scale. If you are willing to sacrifice financial return, your best bet is a small company, because you'll reach your goal more quickly.

But, don't overlook that your greatest satisfaction in that spot will come from achievement, not from big income. You'll probably never earn more than a sizable fraction of what men of equal station will be getting in the giant corporations. Also, you may find yourself working harder than your higher-paid counterparts in the giant firms — men who, again, will not have the same sense of achievement you will enjoy.

So, take your pick . . . but take your time in picking your employer.

Third — Analyze Each Company's
Growth Potential

By now, you have probably narrowed down your search for a career company to one or two firms. You have reached the point of decision. Take a little more time before making your final choice. It will pay off later, in happiness, in financial return, in all-around satisfaction.

Regardless of other factors in the company you choose, you will fare better in a firm that's going places. If ambition spurs you to a high goal, then you will find opportunities opening faster in an expanding company. Even if you're the kind who is inclined to take it easy, you'll invariably draw more money from a company that is growing and showing good profits.

There are several ways to analyze a company's potential.

If the firm is publicly held (common stock available to the public), study its financial history at your library (in such investment books as *Standard & Poor's* or *Moody's Industrials*).

Articles on most big companies are published in the more popular trade journals. Investment publications comment on significant progress of many firms.

Then, of course, an ideal way to get dependable information and reaction is to talk to people who work for the company. They will always tell you the bad points as well as the good points . . . and you'll want to know both. Here are a few specific things you'll want to look for:

1. The company's growth pattern. Has it shown a steady rise in sales over a significant number of years?
2. Are current profits in line with the rest of the industry?
3. How much has the company spent on research? Is the company keeping up-to-date? Business analysts have found from extensive studies that those firms which spend most on research and development usually show the greatest growth in both sales and profits.

Fourth — Find Out Whether The Company
Makes A Practice Of Promoting From Within

Most progressive companies now develop their own executive and supervisory talent. Few go outside to fill key jobs. You'll want to select a company that recognizes its own employees this way.

Any unbiased member of the firm will quickly give you the low-down on this point. And, here is one area where you will not be criticized for asking. Most firms will be impressed when they know you have a lot of ambition for advancement.

But remember, advancement comes only as a reward for outstanding performance. Seniority and promotion are not the same. Promotions must be earned, in most business firms; and you must prepare for promotion — sometimes, years in advance.

Furthermore, promotion almost always comes because somebody up the line has also moved ahead. That's why some men move up fast while others remain in the same old spot year after year. Not only must you prepare for the day when you'll be tapped for greater responsibility, you must also be sure you leave a capable subordinate to take over when you move up.

The young president of a medium-size firm was asked the secret of his rapid rise. "When I started as a salesman," he said, "I made up my mind I would go just as far as I could. Each time I got a promotion, I immediately anaylzed the job just ahead, the place held by my immediate superior. If any phase of his job was unfamiliar to me, I would go to the public library and study up on that subject. I've found that the only way to be sure of steady advancement is to push your boss up the ladder. It's much easier for your boss to move up if everybody knows he has someone ready to fill his shoes in the old job."

So remember, while it is important to select a company which tends to promote from within, the key to rapid advancement still remains with you.

There you have the first four basic steps in selecting your career company. They are:

1. Decide your career objective.
2. Decide whether your objective can best be reached in a small company or a large one.
3. Analyze each company's growth potential.
4. Find out whether the company makes a practice of promoting from within.

Now, the

Fifth Basic Point:
After You Have Selected Your Career Company,
Make Sure That Company Selects You

Now, you're ready for the final and most crucial step. Unless you get the right job in the right company at the right time, all your study and planning will have been to little or no avail. You can take this final step confidently if you have carefully prepared for it.

In the first four basic steps, you've been in the buyer's seat, so to speak. Now, your situation is reversed. Now you have to sell yourself to the company of your choice.

If your prospective company has a specific need for a man like you, and knows of that need, and is advertising for such a man — then you've got it made, as soon as you reply to the ad, have a few interviews, and then fill out the company's personnel forms. It doesn't often happen so easily.

Suppose the company of your choice does not have an opening just now. Suppose nobody in authority in that company has any idea of when there will be an opening. Suppose it's a close-knit firm that's traditionally hard to get into. Suppose you get the well-known cold shoulder every time you get near the company.

Do you sit down and cry?

No.

You'll simply have to create a place for yourself in that firm.

Impossible?

Not at all.

Nearly every company has a place, or will make a place, for any man or woman who can show a profit for the firm over and above the amount it must pay as salary. That's just plain good business. A business cannot afford to turn down your offer to work for it if you can prove that an investment in you will turn a profit for the company.

Then, get busy figuring how to show somebody in that company (somebody in authority) that the company needs to employ you . . . that the company cannot afford *not* to hire you.

If you believe you can build a successful career for yourself in a company that does not seem to have an opening, then you owe it to yourself and to that company to bring your reasons to the company's attention.

Dramatize your worth to the company — your potential worth. There are many ways. The ideal way. of course, is to think up a unique approach.

Here's How One Man Did It

I know the executive vice president of a well-known advertising agency who got his first job by saying to his prospective boss: "I realize you do not know whether I can be helpful to you but I believe I can. So, I'm willing to work without pay until you decide whether or not I am the man for you."

Simple? Yes.

Effective?

He got his opportunity . . . and in a week he was on the payroll.

A small investment of his time resulted in a bright career opportunity. Don't overlook, however, that this young man was prepared for the opportunity before he knocked on the door. He was lucky — if you consider that "luck is where preparation meets opportunity."

Sometimes a novel approach brings an offer to create a job for an imaginative applicant. A young college graduate I knew made a detailed analysis of the home market for power tools. He found that while there was intense competition on many power tools for home use, there was one tool on which a single firm had almost all the business.

He went to another firm that had facilities to produce such an item, and suggested that they develop a competitively priced tool. The company was impressed. The young man was offered a job, immediately . . . though it was many years before the company put that product on the market.

Questions Can Create Interest

It's always possible to create interest in yourself while selecting your career company. My first job was acquired in this way.

I was just out of college. I had nailed down my career objective, and had decided on the size of the company that appeared to offer the greatest opportunity for growth (Steps 1 and 2). However, I still had some doubts about the amount of formal education desirable in my chosen field. I wrote the presidents of several large firms, asking their advice.

Each letter requested an appointment to personally discuss my qualifications. I simply wanted guidance, direct from the experts. I wanted to know whether I needed further university study. I told these corporation heads I wanted their opinions because they undoubtedly were best qualified to give such counsel. (Of course, indirectly but nonetheless effectively, my approach to these big business men was related to my pursuance of Steps 3 and 4.)

To my great satisfaction, I got appointments from all but one of these corporation presidents. Each one I saw advised me to start my business career at once, and each arranged for me to see at least one department head, to discuss job possibilities (whereupon I immediately proceeded with Step No. 5).

What had started out as an exploratory study turned up several very attractive job offers, one of which I accepted gratefully. Thus, a few days after college graduation, I was working at a real opportunity with one of America's largest corporations. My plan was working because I had worked by a plan.

These five basic steps to selecting an ideal career company involve little more than clear, common sense. Yet, it is surprising how many bright young men, and women, will give much less thought to this important subject than they do to the selection of a college, or their first automobile.

Too often they're swayed by offers of higher pay. Too often they decide to join a certain firm simply because a good friend is in that company. Such shallow thinking can be disastrous. Think and act that way, and you may very well find yourself a square peg in a company with nothing but round holes.

Time and effort are all it takes to make a sound decision on your career objective and then locate the most likely company for you. And, it doesn't take very much of either time or effort. It doesn't take much time, compared with the years you'll spend in working out your objective. It doesn't take much effort when you put it against the hard work you'll put in on your chosen job, or jobs, on the way to your ultimate goal.

For years to come, you and your family stand to derive great satisfaction and happiness from the intelligent choice you make now.

For the rest of your life, the measure of your succcess in the area of your main endeavors may hinge on the choice you make now.

Therefore . . . *pick your company carefully* — with the idea that you may very well be head of the firm before you're forty.

3

PLANNED OPPORTUNISM
A "Secret Formula" For Getting Ahead

Planned Opportunism . . . sounds like a direct contradiction, almost. Makes sense, though, when you remember your goal: to become head of the firm before you are forty.

Don't forget: ordinary plans and programs will not work for you. You have set for yourself a most ambitious goal, one almost out of reach for most people. It is a rare person, indeed, who can reach such a position without doing *much* more than what is normal for any ambitious person.

You may become a corporation president just being at the right place at the right time. Some have done it that way. Some corporation presidents will tell you they have been lucky . . . maybe you've heard luck described as "the place where preparation meets opportunity."

Some make it through other circumstances which seem to be accidental; but you cannot depend on lucky breaks to put you in the head man's chair before you are forty.

So, you'll just have to make the breaks yourself. At least, you'll have to be ready for the breaks when they come.

E. W. Scripps, founder of the Scripps-Howard newspaper chain, said: "While luck plays an important part in life, I never knew a fool to have anything but bad luck." Makes sense. So, be wise . . . be ready when Lady Luck knocks at your door . . . and you *will* be ready if your program includes *planned opportunism*.

Chart A Bold And Dramatic Course

You know your objective now . . . we'll assume. You have surveyed the field, thoroughly. You've decided that your best chance of attaining a presidency is in a medium-size firm. That's where your primary talents can be used most effectively. You have landed a job with such a corporation . . . by following the suggestion in Chapter 2.

Following common-sense rules, you have (no doubt) settled on a company whose president will probably retire before you are forty. Also, you are probably figuring that his present management team either does not possess the youthful vitality required for driving the company ahead, or his obvious successor also will retire before you are forty.

Let's say you're now in your late twenties or early thirties. Then, you're figuring soundly, if you are sufficiently thorough in your analysis. It's not only possible, but quite probable, that you'll be top man in that company in the next ten years . . . providing you chart a bold and dramatic course for those all-important years between now and forty. Any course less than bold may lead to mediocrity in your career growth. Any course less than dramatic could leave you in a fairly comfortable but not entirely satisfying middle-level executive position.

What IS Planned Opportunism?

As the phrase suggests, you start with a plan. But your plan must be flexible. You must be able to take advantage of unusual opportunities to show your unusual talents.

Here's how it works:

Suppose you are in Sales. You're a good salesman and you consistently show up at the top, or near the top. You don't meet quotas . . . you beat quotas, regularly. Excellent! But, it's only the beginning.

Not only is it important to show superior sales ability . . . you should start planning *now* to demonstrate your interest in and ability for *other marketing jobs.* While traveling, use your evenings to work out ideas for promotions which, if accepted, will help increase sales. Don't be disappointed if your ideas are not used right away.

It is said of Charles H. Percy (who became President of Bell & Howell at 29) that he came up with new ideas faster than they could be given a hearing. But, happily for young Percy, his organization welcomed good ideas even though it was sometimes many months before they could be activated.

Some companies work six months or a year ahead in planning their promotions. Don't give up if your company does not grab your ideas right away. Even if an idea is rejected entirely, do not despair. You will have put the point across that you have *imagination* and that you're willing to put forth *extra effort* in a field that is not your primary responsibilty . . . and, often, that is more important to your advancement than the idea itself.

Dramatize Your Versatility by coming up with ideas for expanding sales through market analyses which may reveal hitherto untapped potential for your products.

A prominent Government career man I know of got his first big job just that way, about twenty years ago. He made a new-products survey and analysis on steel, as a term paper during his senior year in college. Within weeks after graduation, he was on Big Steel's payroll. His outstanding work, over a period of years, brought a call from Washington, where he has combined public service with private enterprise to a very satisfying degree.

You may see a clever ad by a competitor . . . or even in another field. Don't be afraid to send things like that to your boss, with a comment or two. Such alertness will make you stand out from the crowd as a "real comer."

Always Go Through Channels when you present something. And always find a way to praise your superior and give him credit for putting you on the trail of the idea. The better you make your boss look in the eyes of *his* superiors, the better *you* will look to him. Time and again in your business career, you will observe that the smart assistant pushes his boss up the executive ladder, then follows him up.

Speaking of pushing, I believe it was William Howard Taft who, when he was Chief Justice, gave a word of wisdom to a young attorney, thus: "Young man, there is one word you should always remember. Use it as your constant motto and it will carry you far. That little four-letter word is on the door just behind you." The young man turned to read the word stamped on the metal door-plate: PULL. Just then the Chief Justice continued: "The four-letter word I have in mind is on the *other* side of the door" — and his visitor opened the door to read the word PUSH on the opposite plate.

I believe that PUSH is much more important than PULL, at any point on the executive ladder; but you might as well recognize that there will be times when your superior can, and may, pull you up the ladder with him — especially if you are doing enough *pushing* to make it easy and natural for him to do so.

An example of this PUSH-plus-PULL principle is seen in the

story of Lewis Brown, who became President of Johns-Manville at 35. He was a personnel clerk with Montgomery Ward when his suggestions for increasing efficiency brought him to the attention of President T. F. Meserles. When Meserles was made head of Johns-Manville, he took young Brown with him as assistant. Two years later, when Meserles died, Lewis Brown was ready for the opportunity which put him at the head of a business doing more than $60,000,000 a year.

New Function Can Bring Promotion

Now you have set the stage for promotion within your field of primary specialization. If you have selected a rapidly-expanding company, it is just a matter of time before your ability will be recognized with a promotion.

A fast-growing company always needs junior executives with growth capacity. It may not appear so to a casual observer, but the average small or medium-size company is starving for executive talent, particularly at the lower levels. If an opening for which you feel qualified is slow in coming, you can help it along. One way is to drop a hint about the need for a new department where a genuine contribution can be made to the company's progress.

I know a man who speeded himself up the executive ladder by studying nights for a graduate degree in marketing research. He then sold his company on the need for a department to analyze the market for new products, and set up a long-range program for production planning. His training for this new assignment, combined with his sales experience, qualified him for a higher position. He was soon promoted, and at present he reports directly to the president on matters which vitally concern the company's future planning. His age . . . 33.

Watch Out!

Two things you should watch for when suggesting a new function for yourself:

(1) Be certain there is a genuine need for the function.

(2) Make sure you are qualified for the job.

A miscalculation on either of these points could wash you up as a presidential possibility. So, as Davy Crockett advised, "Be sure you're right, then go ahead."

Steer Clear Of Dead-Ends

Let's say by now you have moved up to a junior executive post.

The most important thing to watch out for at this point: *avoid being side-tracked into a dead-end job.*

Some years ago I knew a young man who had strong qualifications for top management. Reorganization followed the president's retirement, and this young executive was "promoted" to credit manager. He accepted the promotion enthusiastically, as he surely should have done. However, instead of continuing to demonstrate his ability to handle other administrative matters outside the Credit Department, he allowed himself to settle down to the comfortable feeling of a man who has "arrived." ·Actually, he could have gone much further in the company, but his superiors eventually came to look upon him as "good old Charlie . . . dependable as Monday morning . . . as long as he's working on credit matters."

If you find yourself in a dead-end job, you owe it to yourself as well as to your company to show that you have talent beyond the boundaries of your own department. The best way to do this is to discreetly demonstrate your interest in other departments while continuing to do a good job where you are.

For example, if the Credit Department is your blind alley, you you can make up charts to aid Sales in deciding, before a sale is made, who is a good credit risk and who is not. The sales manager will no doubt welcome your suggestions on writing sales memos to his field men, explaining the importance of avoiding sales to customers with weak credit, and showing them how to evaluate such customers.

Sometimes, however, a *discreet* approach will not bring a transfer from the dead-end department, Then, use the *direct* approach. Go directly to your superior. Tell him you feel your job has a limited future, and you would like to be considered for the next opening in another section, where you are qualified.

You'll be surprised at the understanding you'll get from a thinking boss. If your job is truly a dead-end position, he will respect you for recognizing it as such; and he will admire your determination to move ahead. If he is not a thinking person, then you are probably in the wrong company anyway; and the sooner you know it, the sooner you will be able to resume your climb to the top . . . in another firm.

As you employ this very helpful principle of *planned opportunism* in your climb to the top, don't rule out the possible advantages of switching companies . . . as well as gains you might achieve by transferring to another department within your firm. We'll consider this whole subject more fully in a later chapter.

Work With Other Departments

Up to this point, your planning has helped you keep ever mindful of your ultimate goal: the presidency. If you have been working your long-range plan correctly, you've probably made it clear to everyone that your abilities are flexible. By now it's no secret in your company that you do understand and can master, if necessary, the operational functions of any department. You've spread this good impression around by finding numerous opportunities to work closely with all department heads . . . not in an authoritative way, but modestly seeking their help with some of your problems.

Whenever you work with another department, you'll find limitless opportunities to learn about the nuts and bolts of their operation. Sometimes you may even find something that can be improved. But, remember, any suggestions you make must not appear to criticize the top man of that department. It should appear to him that the idea is as much his as yours — something you worked out together to help improve coordination between your area of responsibility and his.

Now you are gaining a wide understanding of the business. You know what happens to an order from the time a salesman sharpens his pencil to the time the merchandise is shipped. The mysteries of procurement and production are no longer outside the sphere of your understanding. Accounting, even though you are not a professional financial man, is no longer something "handled by the boys upstairs." While you could not make up a work sheet if your very life depended on it, at least you know how the work flows through the department, and how it is all accumulated until it finally funnels down and appears as significant data in a financial statement.

You are ready at last, you think, for the big job. Now it's just a matter of waiting for the big break.

Don't Be Fooled

You could not be farther from the truth.

Up to now you have handled many important matters. You have made thousands of decisions and carried to successful completion hundreds and hundreds of vital projects. However, in all your activities you have operated within the framework of established company policy. Perhaps you have influenced policy on occasion, but the final decision was always made by the man who has ultimate responsibility for the success or failure of the corporation.

If that man, the president, makes a mistake on a really big policy decision, it is he who must face the board of directors and explain why the company has failed to move forward.

This is the point at which nine out of ten capable people reach their ultimate level. Few can push beyond this level just below the top. They may not recognize it themselves, but this ceiling is held down firmly by their own lack of an indefinable something that the president has . . . something that makes it easy for a man of presidential caliber to make bold policy decisions .

Again . . . Be Dramatic

If you feel you have the qualifications to deal firmly and confidently with policies than can make or break a company, then you should, at the right time, begin to dramatize that ability.

In every company, there is something in the organizational make-up that could be re-arranged to improve efficiency in every area of operations. It's up to you to find that weakness and sell your top management on the advantages of a change . . . remembering, always, to *do your selling through channels.*

For example, in a very large corporation, which had several different sales departments devoted to the distribution of various subsidiaries' products, a youthful executive in the Marketing Department started campaigning for a single sales force to distribute products of all divisions. After several years of hard selling to every member of the executive committee, he finally won his point. The plan has now been working splendidly for three years, and the young executive (rumor has it) is being groomed for the presidency.

Opportunity Or Side-track?

But suppose, before you've had opportunity to dramatize your qualifications for the presidency, you get an offer to take on an assignment that may take you off your well-planned road toward the top. If you turn it down, the boss will think you do not have the company's interests at heart. And if you take it, you may be out of the eyes of the very people you want to impress with your talents.

My advice to you at such a point is: TAKE THE ASSIGNMENT.

That's where the *opportunism* comes in your program of *planned opportunism.*

You should look on every such challenge as another opportunity to show your mettle. A well-managed company will not bury someone in an assignment if he really has talent that can be used farther up. Chances are, the boys at the top want to see how you'll handle something strictly on your own, where you won't have the day-to-day counsel of superiors to guide you in making decisions.

The president of America's second-largest soap company was using *planned opportunism* when he accepted the post of general manager of his firm's German operation. It didn't look exactly like a promotion at the time . . . but it wasn't very long till he was named president of one of the world's biggest corporations.

David Sarnoff was using *planned opportunism* when, at 19, he stepped down the salary ladder to get a firmer footing with his company, Marconi Wireless.

Young Sarnoff had already worked for Marconi for two years, at $60 a month. He was wireless telegraph operator at the lonely Marconi station on Nantucket Island — an opportunity he grabbed not so much for the money as because this isolated station had a very good technical library. During the two years, he read every book.

Then, Sarnoff got a $10 raise. But he immediately asked for a transfer to Coney Island, at a salary cut. Why? There were no more books where he was. He figured he had learned about all he could on Nantucket Island. Though he could have *earned* more there, he was more interested in *learning*. He knew that he could take a night-school course in electrical engineering at Brooklyn's Pratt Institute if he had a job at the Coney Island station. He got the transfer, and the salary cut.

Going backwards? Not for long. In fact, not at all. At 39, David Sarnoff became President of RCA. He headed the corporation while it became one of the world's largest.

If you're faced with a side-track assignment (or if, like David Sarnoff, you see a real opportunity on a job which looks like a side-track) , then accept it with the firm thought that it's temporary. Always bear in mind that, after you have mastered that problem and discharged it to your credit, you'll work yourself back on course . . . you'll then step up to the next rung, on your sure way to that top rung marked "President."

Never take your eyes off your ultimate goal. You may have to swing and sway with the breezes of corporate necessity, expediency or convenience; but you should not forget, even for a moment, that your destiny points toward the job at the very top of your firm's executive set-up. It's not simple o accomplish all this before you are forty, but it will be just that much easier if you allow *planned opportunism* to work for you.

4

NOTHING WORKS LIKE WORKING HARD

You might think it's really not necessary to point out the importance of hard work. It's obvious, you say. But it is astounding how many people think they are working hard just because they put in a lot of hours on the job.

Ever notice how one person can push out mountains of work with apparent ease, while another works back-breaking hours and accomplishes far less? Sometimes it's the result of a difference in aptitude. Occasionally it's because an emotional or psychological problem causes a mental block. But far too often it's simply because *the individual does not know how to work.*

Learning how to work is not something you can accomplish overnight. However, you may be interested in a few tips to aid you in packing more work into the average day.

While you are going over these points, take time to stop and think for a minute about each one. See if you don't know someone who has made an outstanding success by practicing these principles regularly.

Here are three Steps to More Work . . . Quicker . . . Easier:

First — Plan Ahead And Budget Your Time

Greatest of all time wasters is disorganization. By taking a few minutes each morning, perhaps while dressing, to plan your day, you will be amazed at how much more you'll get done. Sure, you'll have to change your plans once in a while, but the very fact that you have thought out a plan will add an unbelievable amount of orderliness to your working day. Inevitably, this results in a greatly increased rate of productivity.

Second — Let Subordinates Handle Details

If you are to increase your own personal work output, or the production of your department, it is vital to learn early to delegate details of various projects to your subordinates. Whenever you hear someone say, "I do it myself so I know it's done right," you can tell instantly that the man will never reach the top. After all, one man cannot do everything. The very nature of a corporation presidency demands that practically all phases of the company's operation be delegated. So, start learning to delegate.

Third — Use Your Odd Moments

It's told that Horace Greeley, early in his career, developed the habit of using odd moments to accomplish a greater output of editorial writing. Whenever he went out for an interview or an appointment, he always carried a pencil and pad. If he had to wait a few minutes in the outer office of someone he was interviewing, he could be seen busily jotting down notes or making the first draft of an editorial.

I know a very successful corporation executive who has a simple card system for recording thoughts whenever and wherever they occur to him. He keeps blank file cards in his left pocket. When a particular thought comes along, he sets it down on a card, then puts the card in his right pocket. At day's end, he has a number of written thoughts or impressions or facts, ready for transferring to his desk calendar, or dictating for his idea file, or otherwise using so as to save himself time in the long run.

Thomas Edison once said: "Everything comes to him who hustles while he waits." Review Thomas Edison's successes and you'll agree that he knew what he was saying.

In almost every area of business activity, there are many opportunities to use odd moments to increase your output of work. You've seen people studying reports on a train or bus. Some executives have a dictating machine at home, so they can catch up on loose ends at night and on weekends. Others plan their lunch hours and even breakfasts to dispose of conferences that would require time at other, more valuable, hours of the day.

Review those three steps to more work. Are you stepping ahead that way? Can you make every day more productive, and less tiring, by taking those steps?

Relax Now And Then

Now, you may be saying to yourself, "Sure, that's fine; but

don't you want to get a little fun out of life? It sounds as if you're *working* all the time. Isn't there any time for relaxation?"

As a matter of fact, if you are already a hard worker, then you may find yourself with more time for relaxation if you follow those three simple rules. Not only will you find your work output increasing, but you'll have more time for leisure activities.

Sir John Lubbock, Lord Avebury, wrote: "The idle man does not know what it is to enjoy rest. Hard work, moreover, not only tends to give us rest for the body but, what is even more important, peace to the mind."

Your own doctor will no doubt tell you that hurry brings worry . . . and worry brings ulcers. Worry saps strength, but productive, satisfying work produces energy for more work.

Yes, leisure *is* important. If you don't take time out for recreation and rest, you'll soon find your output slipping. Your response to any problem, any situation, will be quicker when your mind and body are well-rested and alert.

Now, being a level-headed individual, you'll not go overboard on this matter of relaxation . . . just as you will be careful not to harm yourself from overwork. Perhaps it will help you to maintain a proper balance if you remember this little ditty by our good friend and mentor, Anonymous:

> Last night I had a funny pain
> And to the Doc I flew.
> Said he, "That comes from overwork,
> There's nothing I can do."
>
> "You need a month of quiet rest,"
> He added, with a smile.
> "You'd better drop your golf and try
> The office for a while."

Be Enthusiastic

Whether you're in the office or out, a proper mental attitude toward work is tremendously important. A much-used rule of thumb is: "If it seems like work, then something is wrong." A friend of mine says he sets his quitting hour at the exact time his work ceases to be fun and starts to be work. His theory is that so long as he loves his job, the only thing that could cause him to become bored or dislike his work is fatigue or staleness.

Maybe you've heard the story of the ditch-digger who was asked by a passer-by: "Well, how do you like your work?"

"Don't like it," replied that man with the shovel; "the harder I work, the lower down in the world I get."

We work and enjoy working hard when we feel we're getting up in the world. And conversely, we make the most rapid and satisfactory advancement in the world of business when we really like what we're doing . . . when we're enthusiastic about it.

Enthusiastic Attitude heads Herman Perl's list of essentials to gaining and holding a sales corporation presidency. Perl should know what it takes, for he heads eighteen different corporations — either as president or as chairman of the board. Companies headed by this 37-year-old dynamo employ some 1,200 salesmen.

Are you ready to put in 73 hours on your job this week? Next week? Every week? That's about what it will take when you become head of your firm.

In the confidential questionnaire addressed to outstanding young corporation presidents, I asked for careful estimates of the average number of hours spent at the job of being head of the firm. Hours were divided between "Direct (Routine)" and "Indirect (Extra-curricular)." Respondents said they spend up to 90 hours per week in "direct, routine" work, mainly at their desks. The average for this category was 57 hours per week.

In "extra-curricular" work connected with the job of president (such as entertaining customers and associates, guest-speaking, civic obligations, planned study) the average was 16 hours per week, year-round. Comes to 73 hours a week working at the job of president . . . and that does not include an hour or two now and then lying awake at night, trying to figure out a solution to some tough problem.

So, be prepared to *work long* as well as *hard when* you become head of your firm.

While You Work Hard, Think

Sidney Weinberg, senior partner of Goldman, Sachs & Company (one of America's great investment banking houses), was asked by Dr. Daniel Starch, "What are the essential qualities for an executive"

Mr. Weinberg, who started his business career at 10, selling newspapers on the Brooklyn waterfront, replied: "I have only one answer and that is *hard work*."[*]

*Reported in Dr. Starch's help-filled volume, *How To Develop Your Executive Ability* (Harper & Bros., 1943, p. 95).

When you closely follow Mr. Weinberg's business career, you soon see that a lot of thinking has accompanied his hard work . . . in fact, it has been a significant part of his hard work.

For example: At 15, he got a job with a Wall Street banking house as runner, at $5 a day. The pay wasn't enough to suit this ambitious lad, so he started thinking how he could earn more. The answer he came up with: more work. So, he soon tripled his earnings by running for two other houses at the same time. It meant three times the work, and it took good figuring to keep his deliveries straight . . . but young Sidney wasn't afraid of hard work, especially when it meant more money. He was giving good service to each of his three employers, and each was well pleased . . . pleased, that is, until each learned he was also working for two other firms. He was fired . . . not once, but three times in a row — bang, bang, bang!

This started young Weinberg to thinking harder . . . not crying. Next day, he decided to start at the top in looking for a job. He went to the 42nd floor of a 42-story office building. He knocked on every door as he came to it. First door: no job. Tenth door: no job. Fortieth floor: no job. Thirty-fifth floor; no job. But he kept on working his way down.

At six o'clock (and quite several floors down), he entered the Goldman, Sachs office, and in a few minutes was hired as a porter's helper. Nineteen years later, at 34, he became a senior partner. For many years he has been one of Wall Street's most active and influential figures, with seats on the New York Stock Exchange and more than a score of corporation boards of directors.

Yes, it's important to combine your hard work with creative thinking. Hard work by itself becomes toil. Hard work combined with creative thinking spells progress.

Thinking Is Hard Work

Arnold Bennett's very successful literary career began with a little book titled *How To Live On 24 Hours A Day*. It will help today's young executives and would-be executives as much as it has helped thousands of others in the last half-century.

In his book, Arnold Bennett says: "As a rule, successful men are by habit comparatively idle."

I disagree with the distinguished writer. If he had put in the word *apparently*, it would make a bit more sense.

How often have you heard a worker say of the president or vice president of his firm: "I sure wish I could spend all *my* day just sitting on my sitter, reading the papers and talking to people; or flying all over the country, seeing the sights and living in those big hotels."

Such is sometimes the *apparent* extent of a high executive's activity — apparent to the worker who cannot see the whole picture. But, if that worker could see the whole picture, he'd recognize that

thinking is just as important as doing . . . and thinking is harder work for most people.

When I talk about *thinking,* I mean straight, hard, analytical, creative thinking. If you want to get acquainted with real hard work, just try it sometime.

You *will* try it as you work your way toward the top . . . for, unlike many successful businessmen of Arnold Bennett's day, the modern corporation executive is a "man on the go." Sure, he takes time to think . . . but even more, he *makes* time to think — at lunch, on planes, in customers' reception rooms; any place, any time he can; and, usually, when other men are daydreaming, "shooting the bull," or just plain relaxing.

A mistake some young executives make is to become too busy to think deep and think straight. Don't get trapped by that mistake . . . a danger we'll consider more thoroughly in later chapters.

Talent Should Be Evaluated

While this book is primarily for those with aspirations for a corporation presidency, I think it is appropriate to pause and comment on one of the great tragedies of present-day American business.

Far too many employees are in jobs to which they neither are suited temperamentally nor have the intellectual aptitude to do a top job. This causes economic waste to both employee and employer and, multiplied by millions of workers, represents an unnecessary increase in company overhead with its inevitable inflation of product costs which consumers must bear, by paying higher prices.

The only way this problem will ever be solved is for industry to develop and use scientific methods for evaluating talents of present and prospective employees. Much progress has been made in use of aptitude tests for industrial job selection. However, these tests still have many flaws and, still worse, they are not used on a wide enough scale.

Don't jump to the wrong conclusion about yourself, just because you might find some parts of your job a bit disagreeable. That does not necessarily mean that you cannot do it, and do it well. Austin Inglehart, former President of General Foods, said: "If you break down almost any job, you will find a large percent of it is disagreeable work. I have never had a disagreeable job in my life, but I have had to do a lot of disagreeable things."

If you feel your work is either tedious or boring, all the time, or if you find yourself wishing you could do something different, chances are you are in the wrong kind of work. You are the only one who can anaylze this situation, however. And, don't kid yourself that you'll like this uninviting work more after that next promotion. Chances are that promotion will never come, because of your attitude . . . or, if it does, it will mean for you just more of the same old grind.

But, if you have a job toward which you have the proper mental attitude, the time you spend will be both fruitful and stimulating. Have you ever lain awake nights thinking about how you can put into effect a new idea that will save or earn your company many thousands of dollars? If you have, you undoubtedly have the correct outlook for your job, and the hours you spend at your work will be satisfying, indeed.

Hard Work Is Important . . .
But It Should NOT SEEM Too Hard

Another of the failures of our present educational and social system is exemplified by college graduates and other young people who seem to think the world owes them a living. Perhaps this is a part of our heritage from recent wars, particularly World War II.

Many veterans have apparently subscribed to the viewpoint that they served their country, so now their country should turn around and serve them. Colleges and universities rushed to welcome ex-G.I.'s, and in many instances made it rather easy for them to acquire academic degrees. We were told that we should try to "understand" these unfortunate young people who were torn away from their normal routine of living and sent to foreign lands where they saw death and destruction at their elbow almost constantly.

While it is understandable that some young people might develop an outlook of this kind, it is absolutely deadly to anyone who wants to grow in the business world. Many, if not most, of the men who have become presidents of their companies since World War II served in various branches of the armed services. I have talked with many of them. I find that most of these veterans are much more interested in understanding themselves and their world, and doing something constructive, than in wanting the world to "understand" and sympathize with them.

One of the most outstanding young corporation presidents I know — he heads several companies — was hospitalized for nine months with serious service-incurred injuries, but you don't hear about it from him — he's too busy being a successful businessman. (The reason I do not mention his name: he would feel embar.-rassed.)

The attitude that "the world owes me a living" is equally damaging in any field of work. Oscar Hammerstein, II, the noted theatrical figure, made this statement:

"Why you were born and why you are living depend entirely on what you are getting out of this world and what you are giving to it. I cannot prove that this is a balance of mathematical perfection, but my own observation of life leads me to the conclusion that there is a very real relationship, both quantitatively and qualitatively, between what you contribute and what you get out of this world."*

To Summarize

Nothing works like working hard.

Hard work is the No. 1 Essential to SUCCESS.

For the up-and-coming executive, working hard includes:

Planning ahead

Budgeting time

Delegating details

Using odd moments — "hustling while you wait"

Relaxing — so you can work harder

Keeping proper mental attitude — "worry kills more people than hard work"

Thinking straight

Getting the best out of people who work with you.

When you learn how to work like that — and when you do it consistently — you'll be on your way to becoming head of the firm, and — if things you can't control so well, fall into line — you'll make it before forty.

---

*Forbes Magazine, October 1, 1958.

5

DON'T BE AFRAID TO BE UNDERPAID
(It Could Be Good For You, In The End)

DANGER: You're getting what you're worth!

That's a sign for the desk of any really ambitious young executive. Yes, one of the most dangerous positions to be in when you are building a career is to be paid exactly what you are worth. You'll become complacent.

So . . . beware!

Take special care to see that you are worth more than you are getting.

True, every job level has a dollar value to a firm. It's also true that most firms try to honestly evaluate the worth of a job, and to compensate the man in that job accordingly. Nevertheless, a man can be worth more to his company than the job classification shows. If he is not worth more, it may take a long time for him to get a crack at the next job up the line.

If a man's salary is in line with his position, and if this is all the man is worth, it is quite likely that he has reached the highest level possible for him in that firm.

Above And Beyond

If, on the other hand, a man is doing a competent job but, by dint of ability and hard work, he contributes to the company's progress above and beyond the requirements of his job, there is no question that he is being paid less than he is worth.

The very fact that he is underpaid will usually assure quicker recognition for a job more in line with his talents . . . providing he is associated with a company that is guided by enlightened management. If he is not in such a company, it may be time for him to take a closer look and decide whether or not he should consider a change.

Correct The Situation

If and whenever you're getting what you're worth, correct that dangerous situation at once.

I cannot imagine when it would ever be smart to correct the situation by asking for a salary cut. You'll *always* be safe when you correct the situation by making yourself more valuable . . . by going that "extra mile," by doing more than your job calls for.

Incidentally, *The Extra Mile* is one of the Seventeen Principles of Business Success set down by Andrew Carnegie. You'll find the Carnegie formula expounded in detail in Napoleon Hill's very helpful volume, *How To Raise Your Own Salary* (published by Napoleon Hill Associates, Division of W. Clement Stone Enterprises, Chicago).

Walter S. Gifford started his climb to the presidency of American Telephone & Telegraph Company by doing more than his job called for. As a young Western Electric payroll clerk, his job was computing piecework payrolls. He got $10 a week, starting soon after college graduation. The work was just plain multiplication and addition, but quite slow and tedious. Young Gifford spent much spare time figuring a faster method — a combination of the decimal and common fraction systems. He got the attention of his superiors by doing this something extra . . . something which soon brought about big savings in his department. This early experience helped Walter Gifford set the pattern for steady progress to the top of the world's biggest corporation.

Cost Clerk To Assistant Production Manager

A small company I know needed a cost clerk. A young man applied, and was put on the payroll at $80 a week. We'll call him Joe . . . since that is not his name, and he'd prefer not to be identified.

A problem developed immediately for Joe. While the job of cost clerk was worth no more than $80 a week, this energetic young man quickly demonstrated an ability that went far beyond the level of work for which he had been hired.

In addition to keeping accurate cost records and pricing each job order for direct labor costs, Joe found ways to bring inconsistencies in production to the attention of management. He pointed out how some jobs could be run more economically by utilizing spare time of girls assigned to another production line. Of course, Joe never could have made such an observation if he had simply sat behind his desk, punching a calculator. He had to make the extra effort to spend some of his spare time in the plant, learning what went into the figures he was using to compute job costs.

Joe had a natural flair for the mechanical. He soon saw how some waste motion could be harnessed to save labor. Before long the production manager suggested to management that this bright young man be given an opportunity to learn something about production. Needless to say, within two years Joe was in charge of Production Scheduling. After a period of seasoning, he was promoted to assistant production manager.

Now, here's the point:

While he was doing the job of cost clerk, Joe was definitely underpaid. He performed beyond the requirements of his job. That's how he corrected that underpay situation. However, it was not good business for the company to pay more for the job than it was actually worth, in spite of his ability and accomplishments. To grant an increase beyond the job's value would have impaired the company's salary structure. Consequently, it was not until he moved up to production scheduler that Joe got a raise. Even then, he was underpaid; and it was not possible to fully reward him until he was made assistant production manager.

I have not checked recently, but I feel certain that our ex-cost clerk Joe is still underpaid. If he is smart, he's glad it's that way. It's to his advantage, because he knows how to take advantage of that kind of situation.

Perspective On Pay Check

Again, a man destined for top-level corporate leadership is seldom preoccupied with thoughts of salary. He is far more interested in how he can help make his company progress and achieve greater earnings. "Monetary incentive" was rated 15th among 23 major factors accounting for the success of a group of American corporation presidents, in a special poll conducted for this book.

This is not to imply that income is ignored by such men. I'm merely pointing up the fact that a businessman with proper perspective will not consider his pay check the most important thing about his work. Necessary, yes; but not most important.

I am prepared to agree with all the writers and philosophers who have echoed the sentiment of Silius Italicus, the first-century Roman who said: "Virtue herself is her own fairest reward." And, while I cannot go along 100 percent with those who hold that "a job well done is its own reward," it certainly is a major, if not *the* major, satisfaction of genuine achievement.

In business, we work for money — among other rewards. If money is your main objective, however, you will probably miss out on these other rewards; whereas, if your main objective is bigger than money, you'll enjoy these other satisfactions plus money.

I believe the proper perspective on your pay check can be best gained by the person who tries to adopt, at least to some degree, the philosophy expressed by Jesus of Nazareth when he advised: "Seek ye *first* the kindom of . . . righteousness, and all these things shall be added unto you."

If modern examples are needed: read the story of "Golden Rule" Nash . . . or of P. P. Hove, the Minneapolis grocer who set up his business with the determination to apply the Golden Rule to his customers. His store expanded into one of the nation's outstanding supermarket chains.

Or, consider the career of Ernest E. Norris, who rose from telegrapher to President of the Southern Railway, and whose concern was first, last, and always, the welfare of the customer. Or the corporate history of Ralston-Purina Company, which is largely the lengthened shadow of Founder William Danforth, whose dominating philosophy was:

STAND TALL (Health)
THINK TALL (Good Mental Attitude)
SMILE TALL (Be a Good Human Being)
LIVE TALL (Religiously)

These and hundreds of other outstanding successful American men of commerce have been rewarded handsomely, in money and material things . . . but if you'll read their histories carefully, you'll find that money was not uppermost in their minds.

The fact that higher and higher income usually follows a man of this kind throughout his career is a tribute to the American free enterprise system. No matter what his income level, any American can be proud of the general way in which our industrial structure rewards those individuals who have the ability and who are willing to take on the responsibilities necessary to help a firm grow.

But to the man himself, the constantly increasing size of his personal estate is often incidental to the bigger job of carrying out expansion plans which are the products of his own imagination —

supported, of course, by plenty of hard work in the form of straight thinking. This incidental role of money explains why some executives are forever turning down offers from bigger firms at higher salaries. They simply cannot leave a job half-done. To them, the satisfaction of seeing a dream develop into reality means more than a salary two or three times larger. They are at least halfway in agreement with Emerson. To them, at least a considerable part of "the reward of a thing well done, is to have done it." In addition to money, they get a deeper satisfaction.

Rewards Besides Salary

Partly because of this principle, and partly because of the present high tax rate, more and more firms have turned to ways other than higher salaries to reward their top executives. Many firms try to hold down the salaries of their officers, and set up stock options or pension plans instead. Not only does this reduce the amount of tax a man must pay on current income, but it ties his rewards directly to any future results he may achieve, and to the company's growth to which he will have opportunity to contribute.

This makes a great deal of sense to a man who has the right outlook. Why shouldn't he take a smaller salary now and let the victory he hopes to win in the future provide him with his major material rewards?

The executive with this kind of foresight and ability is willing to take his chances on his own capacity to produce results. If he loses, the prize will not be there. If he wins, his victory will bring a double reward of satisfaction and financial growth. And to the average executive of great ability, this sense of satisfaction will be as important as, or even more important than, his material reward.

To Summarize

If money is your main goal, you'll probably make less. Don't let $$ blind you to opportunities. Always make yourself worth more than your pay.

> Don't be afraid
> to be underpaid;
>> it could
>> be good
>>> for you . . .
>>> in the end.

6

EXPERIENCE TAKES TIME —
CLIMB UP FASTER ON OTHERS' EXPERIENCE

Benjamin Franklin: "Experience keeps a dear school, but fools will learn in no other."

Oscar Wilde: "Experience is the name everyone gives to his mistakes."

Henry Ford: "If money is your only hope for independence, you will never have it. The only real security that a man can have in this world is a reserve of knowledge, experience and ability."

Joseph Collins: "A prudent man profits from personal experience, a wise one from the experience of others."

Borrowing good thoughts from these thoughtful, and successful, men of experience and wisdom, we may logically conclude:

> *He who would profit* MOST *from experience* MUST *profit from the experience of others.*

When you put great store in the experience of others, then:

. . . if Franklin was right, your experience (and *knowledge,* which is equivalent to second-hand experience) costs you less;

. . . if Oscar Wilde was right, you'll make fewer mistakes;

. . . if Henry Ford (the world's first billionaire) was right, you need never worry about money;

. . . if Dr. Joseph Collins was right, why not follow the injunction he suggests? That's what today's fastest-rising young executives are doing . . . they are using second-hand experience; it's just as good, if you'll use it!

Experience is the bridge between Ambition and Achievement. If somebody else has already built that bridge . . . why not cross over on it rather than build a bridge of your own?

The Arabs have a proverb: "No man is a good physician who has never been sick."

That proverb may have been a good enough guidepost for an ancient day. Modern medicine is daily proving it wrong. Yes, in today's great medical centers . . . and even in the humblest sick-rooms . . . second-hand experience (dependable, sure *knowledge*) works more and greater miracles than all the painstaking, palliating predecessors of Hippocrates. The corollary holds for modern business.

You, as a young executive, should never forget that you are still young. Remember, you are younger than other executives. Learn from *their* experience . . . and you won't have to spend so much of your time and so much of yourself in making your own mistakes.

Keep Your Mouth Shut

It won't be easy.

Too many otherwise promising young executives mistakenly think they can create a good impression by continually making themselves heard. They're forever spouting *their* opinions and ideas. They do this in the face of differing thoughts from older executives who have often been through the very same problems. They won't listen to the Voice of Experience (of others). They seem determined to waste everyone's time with fruitless conversation long after the facts necessary to a conclusion are obvious to others.

"Nothing is opened by mistake so often as some people's mouths," I've heard it said.

Though you may not yet be a "wise old bird," for heaven's sake (and, more particularly, your own sake) don't be a magpie. That's not the way to get ahead in business.

You'll never convince your superiors that you have the desire and qualifications for unlimited growth unless you actively seek the advice and counsel of older men who are in a position to guide your thinking. There's an old English proverb: "Better to slip with the foot than with the tongue." Nothing will turn the stomachs of your superiors quicker than an unbridled torrent of verbal nonsense . . . an uninhibited display of theory from a man obviously not qualified to express an opinion.

So . . . keep your mouth shut — but keep your eyes and ears, and mind, open.

Seek Expert Advice

Remember, this is the day of specialization. No one — not even a top corporation executive — is expected to know everything about everything. That's why the most successful corporation presidents surround themselves with experts. The head of the firm must have around him a team of specialists — in accounting, advertising, personnel, production, and so on.

I have sat in the office of the chairman of the board of a quarter-billion-dollar corporation while he called half a dozen experts before making a decision. He would not think of signing a financial contract without first consulting with both an attorney and a financial specialist. And, under our modern tax structure, it is very probable he would call in a tax expert, to boot.

Sir William Temple, the 17th-century English statesman, once said: "The best rules to form a young man are: to talk a little, to hear much, to reflect alone upon what has passed in company, to distrust one's own opinions, and value others that deserve it."* Wise words for anyone to heed, but especially valuable for a young person who wants to climb fast in a modern corporation.

Another Advantage

While the obvious and primary value of seeking advice from older executives is the experienced, proven information you will get, there is also another advantage which can be even more valuable to you.

Every person likes to have others feel that he knows a great deal about the work he's doing. Asking for advice demonstrates (to the person asked) your realization that he is somewhat of an authority. Often, it creates a feeling of warmth toward you. Furthermore, if you take the advice you have asked for, you will have a strong supporter in your corner when your program or your policy comes up for discussion.

Hence, as a corollary benefit, you can use your habit of advice-seeking as a means of getting close to higher-level executives. You should never be insincere, however, in your associations with these mentors. A phony approach will always be recognized. You'll fare

---

*Quoted in *Forbes* Magazine, October 1, 1958.

better if you develop a genuine interest in the opinions of men who are obviously in a position to help you immeasurably with your problems.

A Few More Words From THE VOICE OF EXPERIENCE:

Edmund Burke: "He who calls in the aid of an equal understanding doubles his own; and he who profits by a superior understanding raises his powers to a level with the heights of the superior understanding he units with."

Samuel Taylor Coleridge: "Advice is like snow; the softer it falls, the longer it dwells upon, and the deeper it sinks into the mind."

Goethe: "To accept good advice is but to increase one's own ability."

When You Do Open Your Mouth . . .
LET A QUESTION COME OUT

I know a middle-level executive who is always asking questions, no matter where he happens to be. If he is attending a meeting where more experienced officers are discussing a matter with which he is not familiar, his face shows complete absorption in what others are saying. After such a meeting, he always asks questions of certain individuals. He wants to know why Mr. X said this, or how Mr. Y arrived at his conclusion. Once I heard him say, "I could sit all day and listen to Mr. Z discuss financial matters."

This rising executive *takes* advice, too. That's one way he increases his own ability. I was on a sales call with him. He asked advice of the buyer, on the wording of a sales sheet. Back at his office, he immediately dictated an order to the Art Department to change copy along lines suggested by this buyer. Perhaps it is no coincidence that this young man, age 36, is presently a vice president of a corporation doing some $750,000 a year. He reached this position after less than a year with the corporation.

Thomas Roy Jones, a country boy who rose to the top of Daystrom, Inc., was addressing a trade convention: "You're looking," said he, "at a man who has made a career of being dumb, and thinks it makes sense . . . I call the experts and ask questions. Then I take action on the other fellow's advice and get a reputation for being smart, and am invited to come to conventions and make speeches to the fellows from whom I obtained the answers."

Lammot duPont once said: "There's one trick about management that I learned early. It is to surround yourself with men who know more than you do, and listen to them."

In Miami, Florida, there's another DuPont — W. H. Jr. — who (in 1959) was head of ten different companies while still an undergraduate at the University of Miami. President W. H. DuPont, Jr., age 22, employed one of his professors. Like Lammot DuPont, he is surrounding himself with "men who know more."

Philip D. Armour, whose name is synonymous with meat throughout the Western Hemisphere, is quoted: "Most of my success has been due to keeping my mouth shut."

> It's worth repeating: Keep your mouth shut, most of the time . . . but keep your eyes and ears and mind open . . . and seek advice from experts.

It's done by successful corporation heads. How much more important for you, on your way to becoming head of the firm!

Know Where To Get Information

The day of the flamboyant Mr. Know-it-all is just about over. A decade or two ago it was traditional for an executive to try to overwhelm his subordinates, and even his superiors, with his great knowledge of the operation. Not now.

In today's era of business diversification, practically no one is expected to carry all the details of a business in his head. Rather than trying to impress people with his encyclopedic brain, the modern executive concentrates on knowing where the information can be found and assembled. Result: an entirely new personality for the executive. Even at the top, the best executives spend as much time listening as they do telling people what to do.

I can still picture the president of a company I once worked for. He leaned back in his chair, sucking on his pipe, asking pin-sharp questions designed to get the facts about a project I was recommending. Few words were wasted. After I had completed my explanation, he grasped the typewritten report and without further comment simply wrote "O.K." on it. Then, after scribbling his initials, he handed the report back to me . . . all ready for action.

Of course, this is not to imply that there are not times when you must become quite vocal in support of, or in opposition to, something on which you have a firm conviction. Nor is it to suggest that you should not develop your talents for verbal communication. A good speaking voice and experience in "thinking on your feet" are invaluable assets. These are important qualifications for a man who must have the strength for continued career growth.

However, there is a time to speak up . . . and a time to listen.

You cannot go far wrong if you develop the habit of listening with genuine interest whenever you have an opportunity to get free advice from older executives. Remember, they've spent many years acquiring and sharpening their tools-of-the-trade, *Knowledge* and *Experience.*

You must have these tools and be quite familiar with their use before you are forty . . . if you are to become head of the firm while you're still 39, or younger..

7

CULTIVATE SINGLENESS OF PURPOSE

Many talented men and women have the desire and ability to get ahead. Yet, they never quite make the grade. Why?

Indefinite purpose.

Scattered effort.

Often, this failure to make the grade comes from lack of complete absorption in one's job. As a general rule, these people who *almost* reach the mark come just a little bit short because they let other things, no matter how worthy, interfere with their forward movement. They get side-tracked too often and too long.

Once again, let me emphasize that achieving a corporation presidency before you're forty will take more than normal ambition, and you must hold fast to principles which most men would not be willing to embrace. If you have determined to try for the top job, and if you are sincere in your willingness to make reasonable sacrifices to achieve your goal . . . then you may be psychologically attuned to pursue a course which some have termed *singleness of purpose*.

Benjamin Disraeli, British Prime Minister, was both in and out of power during the long reign of Queen Victoria. His "downs" and "ups" in government lend significance to these words he wrote in later life:

"The secret of success is constancy to purpose."

What IS Singleness Of Purpose?

It means simply that your personal philosophy allows very little interference with your program to prepare yourself for and earn for yourself a company presidency.

Turning down an evening of dancing at the country club is seldom easy. It could enhance your popularity . . . a lot of the "right people" will be there, surely.

It's tough to say "No" to your neighborhood gang when they're planning a week-end of fishing. But you have to put the finishing touches on a report for the boss. So, you say "No." The self-discipline you show at such times will mark you as a man destined for corporate leadership.

Early in my career, I had an interview with the President of Nopco Chemical Corp., Mr. Charles P. Gulick. He was telling me a few things about himself and his ideas on how to get ahead in business. To demonstrate a point closely akin to what I call *singleness of purpose,* he told me of a personal experience he had when Contract Bridge was gaining popularity.

"All my friends were playing the game," Mr. Gulick said. "I, myself, very much liked to sit down and spend an evening playing a few rubbers. One day, however, I woke up and discovered that I was spending more time playing bridge than I was reviewing financial reports from our various subsidiaries. I made up my mind right then that it was either Contract Bridge or my Company. From that day on, I never played another game of bridge."

A bit extreme, you think? But remember, you will need an extreme program if you are to gain and hold a job of top corporate responsibility.

Keep Your Eye On Your Target

I related a story in Chapter 1 about a youthful corporation president who lost his job after trying to work his way into politics. He could not do justice to either of these responsibilities because he was trying to handle both . . . he was spreading himself too thin for effectiveness in either job.

This ex-president had practiced the principle of *singleness of purpose* when moving up the corporate ladder; but, as soon as he reached the top, he discarded this principle, at least partially. Consequently, he was unable to meet his responsibilities to his company. This, probably more than any other single factor, was the cause of his decline and fall.

The successful corporation president cannot, I believe, leave business at the office . . . at least, not as a general rule. While he recognizes the value of proper balance between work and recreation, the weight of his activity is always in favor of work . . . at the office, at home, or elsewhere.

This apt story is told of Robert W. Woodruff, who became President of The Coca-Cola Company at 34. Traveling through Georgia (where Coca-Cola was born), he stopped at a crossroads store for a cold drink of some kind (make your own guess). While standing at the red-and-white cooler with the familiar frosty bottle in one hand, he emptied out the container of bottle caps and counted the Coke caps against all others. He was "on the job" even while pausing for refreshment.*

Make Your SPARE TIME, STAIR TIME

The stairway to success in business is marked by successive platforms or plateaus. The distances between these ever-higher levels of accomplishment are achieved only through the *extra* effort of the individual. Today you are a foreman. There's little or no chance that you'll be superintendent next year unless *you* do something about it . . . and a lot of what you'll have to do will have to be done on *your* time, not on company time.

You're already working longer hours than average. Most ambitious young executives do. Still, it might amaze you to find that four to eight hours every day are taken up in essential but non-productive activities: eating, dressing, riding to work, simply walking to and from your appointments.

Most people use this time to think . . . and that's good. But what do most people think *about* in this spare time? Gardening. Fishing. Repairing the house. How to lick the shirt off Sam Slick in next Wednesday night's poker game. These are just some of the items ordinarily on a person's mind during those hours when he is not actively at work on the job.

On the other hand, if a person is living the principle of *singleness of purpose,* then it's quite likely that he uses most of these spare moments to *think creatively* about his work. A successful business man once told me, "Just as soon as my feet hit the floor in the morning, I'm thinking about business."

Henry L. Doherty, who started as an office boy and later organized Cities Service Company, once said: "The young man who spends his spare moments with greatest profit to himself will be able to sell his working hours in later life at the greatest profit."

Learn To Think Anywhere

Pat, the well-known Irish character, had never been to the zoo.

---

*Reported in *Hartwell* (Ga.) *Sun.*

So, one Sunday afternoon, friend Mike took him to see the monkeys. Before arriving, Mike gave quite a build-up to a big black monkey . . . a free-swinging simian who was, usually, quite a cut-up on the trapeze. When they arrived, most of the frisky beasts were cavorting all over the place, just like monkeys are supposed to do. But the big black fellow just sat there and looked right back at Pat and Mike, like a taciturn purchasing agent.

"So that's the big frisky fellow you've been ravin' about?" questioned Pat.

"Shure, and he's the one," said Mike.

"Begorra if he ain't a-layin' down on the job today."

"He's nothin' o' the sort!" retorted Mike.

"An' how're ye figurin' that?" Pat pressed him.

"Well, maybe he don't look to be too busy now," Mike came back, "but can't you see, he's doin' a devil of a lot o' thinkin'."

Real thinking is hard work. At least, it's that way for human beings. But it pays off . . . in business and in every other sphere. One of the big problems in our present-day business complex is that executives are so busy with administrative problems they do not have enough time to think and plan.

Edward H. Harriman, the railroad king, walked into the office of a junior executive. The man was reared back in his swivel chair, feet on desk, arms crossed on his chest, gazing at the ceiling. The young man quickly straightened up, and tried to open his mouth (with visions of a hasty firing, no doubt, dancing through his brain) . . . but he was speechless. Harriman relieved the situation smoothly. As he turned and headed out the door, he turned and remarked, "Well, Jones, I'm glad to see you taking time to think."

Using odd moments is just one more way to put into your personal make-up that little *plus* that will allow you time to think creatively . . . thereby making greater contributions to your firm, which is the best possible way to advance yourself.

Singleness Of Purpose Will Show

Singleness of purpose reveals itself in many little ways. If you become restless when it's necessary for you to attend a social function, you've got it . . . that is, if you grow restless because the topics of conversation do not bear on your work or your business in general. If you find yourself enjoying the company of other businessmen more than people who do not like to discuss economics or business trends, then you've got it.

I'll never forget the first social function I attended in a large firm I had just joined. Most of the officers were there, with their wives. After dinner, we all retired to the living room. The wives gathered at one end, husbands at the other.

The only conversation I heard all evening from any of the men was about business. They talked about our company, and prospects for the future. They talked about our competitors. They talked about our customers. They even talked about the general economic outlook and current activity on the stock market.

Always, the conversation was on subjects that affected, or could affect, our firm. Here was a group of men who were all practicing *singleness of purpose*. Not because it was required of them, but simply because, to them, their company and its business were the most important things in their lives.

Maintain Balance

Don't let me paint a lopsided picture. I should qualify these remarks with one other thought:

Balance is necessary. The difference between the top executive and the average worker is a matter of degree. Andrew Carnegie said it this way; he told Princeton University students that the way to get to the top in business is to "conduct your business with just a little more ability than the average man in your line."

You should have a vital interest in your family, of course, and in one or two outside interests or hobbies . . . any constructive interest that takes your mind off yourself and your business problems now and then.

"Happy marriage and moral support at home" ranked 3rd among 23 qualities which a group of corporation presidents rated as factors contributing to their rise. Mention that to your wife, sometime . . . and don't forget to thank her for all the help she has already given you, in countless ways.

Rest Is MEANS, Not END

Activities such as your participation in trade association, fraternal and club programs — such activities can be recreational to a degree. They help you clear your mind, by getting it off yourself. They widen your view. They renew the whole man. They *re-create* energy, enthusiasm, strength.

Recreation is necessary. The person who practices *singleness of purpose*, however, will use periods of recreation and rest as a means to an end, rather than an end in itself. He knows that he will be able to perform better if he takes time out now and then to rebuild his strength and sharpen his mind for tomorrow's problems.

The difference between this kind of wise executive and the one who is just average is that the average man cannot wait to finish the job at hand so he can enjoy some kind of play, or at least an activity divorced from his work. He's the kind of businessman-patient to whom the doctor said, in Chapter 4: "You'd better drop your golf and try the office for a while."

Not everyone can put his job before nearly everything else in his life. Life just isn't set up that way, and most people aren't made that way. But a person who is willing and able to practice this kind of *singleness of purpose* is often the person who will, someday, find his name near the top of the list of his company's officers . . . and there's a good chance he'll be head of the firm before forty.

8

LEARN ALL YOU CAN
(Especially About Your Own Firm)

The more you learn, the more you'll earn . . . as a general rule. In business, this fact is even more significant and important than in most other fields.

Formal education is beneficial but not requisite to advancement in business . . . as witness the record of Frederick H. Ecker, for many years the guiding hand of Metropolitan Life Insurance Company. Young Ecker went to work full-time as soon as he finished grammar school (near the top of his class). But his schooling didn't stop just because he had a job. He immediately began studying accounting in night school. For many, many years he spent a major part of his own time studying. "Instead of working my way through college," he said, when president of the world's largest insurance company, "I colleged my way through work.*

Another highly successful businessman who "colleged his way through work" was Charles E. Wilson, former President of General Electric.† He left school at 12, but studied in night school and took correspondence courses intensively until he was 25.

You'll find many such examples in the annals of business . . . men who never stopped learning, though their formal schooling ended a bit early. Here are a few:

---

*Quoted in Daniel Starch's excellent book, *How To Develop Your Executive Ability* (Harper & Bros., 1943), a book so filled with meaty fare for the ambitious young businessman that you'll have trouble closing it before you read to the end.

†Another CHARLES E. WILSON was head of General Motors at about the same time. GM's Wilson became Secretary of Defense in President Eisenhower's Cabinet.

BENJAMIN FRANKLIN
HENRY FORD
JOHN D. ROCKEFELLER
WALTER P. CHRYSLER
ANDREW CARNEGIE
GEORGE M. PULLMAN
WILLIAM COLGATE . . . *toiletries*
JAMES B. DUKE . . . *tobacco*
E. H. HARRIMAN . . *Union Pacific Railroad*
JAMES J. HILL . . . *Great Northern Railway*
ISAAC M. SINGER . . . *sewing machines*
JOHN WANAMAKER . . . *merchant and Postmaster General*
FRANK W. WOOLWORTH . . . *variety stores*

Nowadays, it is not unheard of for a Ph.D. to head a business firm. This is especially true in "glamor" industries such as astronautics, electronics, and nuclear energy, where great technical skill is required of nearly every worker, from janitor up. Heads of many such firms hold impressive degrees from leading universities. Many of them have learned, and are learning, management techniques through on-the-job study, and through study courses and seminars offered by such organizations as American Marketing Association, American Management Association and the Young Presidents Organization.

Half a dozen or more leading publishers offer not only a continuous flow of readable "how-to" books on all phases of business, from accounting to zoning, but also mail-order and correspondence courses in the more popular subjects, such as letter-writing, personnel management, selling, and so forth. If you're a coming young executive, your name is perhaps already on the mailing lists of such publishers. Here are just a few of the leaders in this field:

BOOK PUBLISHERS:
Printer's Ink Publishing Company
McGraw-Hill
Harper & Row
Prentice-Hall
Ronald Press (specializing in accounting)
D. Van Nostrand Company
Executive Book Club

PUBLISHERS OF COURSES:
American Management Association

Dartnell Company
National Research Bureau
LaSalle Extension University
Alexander Hamilton Institute
International Correspondence Schools

Learn With A Purpose

Since your goal is crystal-clear to you, and since you are taking the most direct route to your goal, you will pass up a lot of attractive opportunities to learn, more about your line of business. You *must* pass up many such opportunities in favor of concentrated study on matters *directly* concerned with your own firm, *directly* concerned with the work you're now doing or will be doing in your next job, *directly* in line with your goal. Books, magazines, and other informational material of a corollary nature would be interesting, and even helpful . . . but you'll have to select the ones which offer you the greatest benefit for the least expenditure of time, money, and attention.

In one of his essays, the 18th-century Irish-English writer Richard Steele says that "learning is not knowledge, but rather the art of using it." This is the view for the practical businessman. Everything you learn should be learned for use, and not just to show others how much you know.

Practical knowledge is, of course, the greatest factor in personal growth. When you stop learning, you'll stop growing . . . as a person and as a businessman. You'll keep on learning if you bear in mind Thomas a Kempis' observation that a man should remember "that what he knows is but a very little in comparison of what he is ignorant of."

Random reading is not time wasted if, now and then, you garner a fact or thought you can put to use. But you'll learn more, quicker, if you have some kind of plan. Decide which newspapers, which magazines, which trade publications offer you the most "meat" . . . and let all the others go with just a hasty look now and then.

Go to bed with a book, occasionally. Detective stories and novels are sometimes relaxing — and helpful to that extent but most dynamic business men I've talked with on this matter say they enjoy a pertinent biography much more. The lives of yesterday's business leaders make real spicy reading, sometimes. You'll find such books in your public library, by the dozens. And, you can read about today's business leaders in your newspaper as well as in trade magazines.

Yes, read with a purpose, remembering that *the more you learn, the more you'll earn.*

Learn Your Firm's Operation, A—Z

You may be a real whiz of a salesman . . . but unless and until you show some interest in and knowledge of fiscal matters, you won't be a management man. You may be the shrewdest accountant your firm ever saw . . . but unless and until you know something about personnel management, you won't climb very far up the executive ladder.

The head of the firm is severely handicapped if he does not have *some* firsthand knowledge of every phase of his company's operation. It may be fifteen years before you'll be sitting in the president's chair, but the firsthand knowledge you gain this summer about another department than your own (perhaps by filling in for somebody on vacation) will be useful when you do get there. Don't pass up any opportunity to learn something about what's going on in other departments . . . and *how* and *why.*

Chapter 3 suggests several ways of opening doors into other departments. One of those ways is worth repeating, I think: *modestly seek the advice and help of heads of other departments with some of your problems.* There's no smoother or more effective way, usually, to begin learning something about the other department. Naturally, your seeking of advice and help will be sincere. The head of that other department will feel complimented, and one day he'll probably return the compliment by seeking some advice and help from you.

To repeat another important point: *always go through channels.* Don't erect roadblocks to your own progress by getting your immediate superior feeling offended.

Learn To Open Doors

In addition to learning about every other department in your firm, through "helping out" and through seeking advice there, you may be able to *make* other opportunities to learn more about what's going on at top level and other levels.

Let's say photography is your hobby, and it happens that the head of your firm is also a shutterbug. Maybe you can cultivate a closer relationship around that mutual interest. Or maybe you're a "barber shop" singer . . . a bird watcher . . . a daisy picker.

Some presidents are real "bugs" about their hobbies. If the president of your firm is that way, don't overlook the opportunities this may open for you . . . but, don't strain yourself on this score; any such relationship should be natural and genuine.

If you are in a small or medium-size firm, there's an almost sure-fire way to learn a lot about every department. In most such firms, everybody is and always has been so busy that nobody has set down a history of the company. When a firm becomes big enough to have a Publicity Department, that's one of the first projects. But, if your firm isn't yet that big, and if nobody has attempted to assemble the interesting historical facts about your firm . . . there's a wide-open opportunity for you to establish some very interesting contacts with every department head, every officer — even every director and major stockholder if you want to go that far. Just suggest the project to the head of your firm and tell him you'd like to do it — mostly on your time, of course. You'll get attention, if not an immediate O.K. Even if your proposal is turned down, you will have made an impression that can't do anything but good for you.

Not only will such a project spotlight you as a "comer" in the eyes of present management . . . even more important, it will give you invaluable appreciation of problems which have faced your firm's management up to now, and this understanding will be immeasurably useful as you get nearer and nearer to being head of the firm, before forty.

9

BECOME AN EXPERT IN SOMETHING
It Will Open Doors Quicker Than You Think

The first step up the executive ladder is often the most difficult. Once you've got the attention of management enough to secure that first big promotion, you have a good chance at continued growth and steady advancement.

But how do you come to the attention of management in the first place?

Many ways.

One sure-fire technique is to *become an expert in something*. If there is a subject in which you are particularly interested, and if your company can use a person well-versed in that subject, then you can get favorable attention by making a thorough study of the field and letting it be known that your knowledge is available. That process calls for salesmanship, of course. It's the kind of subtle salesmanship used every day by successful executives.

How George Did It

George is a successful executive I've known for some years. He started as a young clerk in a company which was planning to raise additional capital via a public stock issue, just about the time when the Securities and Exchange Commission was enacted into being. SEC rules and regulatons were numerous and confusing. The SEC was too new for even the attorneys to know all the answers. Partly because George was interested in the whole problem of public financing, and partly because he saw an opportunity to be of service to his company and himself, he studied the SEC regulations until he was virtually an expert on the subject.

Soon, key executives were coming to George for advice and interpretation of certain rules and regulations of the SEC. Eventually, even the president of the corporation learned of the young man's mastery of the subject, and frequently called on him for counsel.

Thus, in a most dramatic way, George had brought himself before management and demonstrated a keen understanding of how the new regulations would affect his firm's plans. This was no small accomplishment for a youth in his early twenties. Needless to say, it put him in line for a promotion.

Opportunities like that are opening up all the time. The Federal Government is constantly passing new laws which affect business one way or another. A knowledge of these laws based on detailed study can often be of great help to your company in developing its future policies.

Look Away . . . Across The Sea

If your firm does not have an active foreign department, and yet your products could be sold abroad, just think of the contribution you might make by becoming a quasi-expert in Exporting.

I once stumbled on a casual statement in an economics book, concerning the favorable tax climate in Puerto Rico. This was before the intensive advertising and promotional program by the Puerto Rican Government. I studied up on the possibilities of manufacturing in Puerto Rico and, after I was sure of my facts, I presented a recommendation to management. It was received with enthusiasm, and within six weeks I was on my way to Puerto Rico with our corporation attorney to look for a plant site.

Expert In Employee Selection

I know an up-and-coming executive in one of the nation's larger drug manufacturing concerns. When he came to the firm's home office, less than eighteen months ago, he recognized a weakness in the company's employee selection policies. Because he believed he could make a genuine contribution, he made a study of aptitude tests and how they were being used in industry.

Before long, aptitude tests were being used in the Sales Department. Now my friend is known throughout the company as an expert on employee selection and testing. Small wonder he is already assistant to the vice president and director of sales.

Spread The Word Around

Sometimes your reputation as an expert will spread outside your own company. This can be valuable to you, and to your firm.

At one time I worked for a company whose primary business came from the drug trade. After a few years with this concern, I noted a gradual shift in sales pattern from drug stores to supermarkets.

Since our products were primarily non-food items, I decided to delve deeper into the exciting new field of selling non-food products through grocery outlets. Such merchandising was then in its infancy.

The study was fascinating. It revealed trends I had never dreamed existed . . . except possibly with our own line, where a definite swing from drug to food stores was evident.

I wrote an article for a marketing journal, entitled "Merchandising Non-Food Items Through Food Stores." Later I was asked to write other articles. Eventually I was invited to be a consultant on non-foods at a national trade association convention. Undoubtedly, this boosted the prestige of my company in the eyes of the retailers, and I can't help thinking it influenced some favorable comment toward me by my superiors.

Even after you have come to the attention of management, a reputation for being an expert in some field will help sustain interest in you as possible growth material. What a boost to your prestige to be called into a meeting of the executive committee or the board of directors, to give an opinion on a subject in which you are particularly well versed. I have seen this happen to young men, and women too. You can almost hear the unspoken thoughts of executive after executive as they inwardly speculate, "I'll bet that young person will be in a much bigger job ten years from now."

Stand Out From The Crowd

Becoming an expert in something points up again the underlying principle behind a program for reaching the presidential level before forty. Your career cannot be ordinary or conventional in any way. If it is, you'll simply be one of the crowd and then you'll be competing solely on the basis of ability and the breaks.

Presumably, your associates will have ability equal to or nearly equal to your own. Also, the law of averages dictates that they will have as many lucky breaks as you. You must create an impression of yourself that will pull you up beyond the level of the crowd. Being an expert in a specific field of some value to your firm is one more way to accomplish this objective.

The Expert Makes Impressions, Everywhere

Occasionally, an expert will come into a firm from the outside and because of the great need for his knowledge he will have a meteoric rise.

I recall one instance in which an Internal Revenue man came into a firm through a routine audit of its tax returns. The company's management was so completely impressed with this man's knowledge that they later contacted him and asked him to join the firm as tax advisor. Within two years he was controller, and later became treasurer. Before he was forty, he was named president, and he has held that top position for twenty-two years.

Don't Lose The Big Picture

I recall a comment by Henry Ford, II, who came to the head of his family's great industrial empire at 28: "Mass production . . . produced the difficult problem of specialization, where the individual loses sight of the social usefulness of what he does."

Too much specialization is also apt to cause the individual to lose sight of important developments, and opportunities, in his own firm. While becoming an expert in some particular phase of your firm's operation, do not become blinded to what's going on in other departments. Don't get lost in the forest by sticking too close to your own tree. Don't lose the larger picture.

It goes without saying, you should have complete mastery of your own job, and as well-rounded an understanding of your entire company as you can. However, if you'll go that extra mile and put forth the effort to become an expert in an additional field of value to your company, you may find doors opening to you beyond your wildest dreams. It certainly will help you get the notice of management, and it could be your first big step toward becoming head of the firm before forty.

10

BE A CONTROLLER, WHATEVER YOUR TITLE
Cost-Consciousness Is Always Vital

If I were to say to you, "The primary purpose of any business is to make a profit," you would no doubt reply: "That's obvious."

Some executives don't agree, apparently. Yes, you'll find top-level executives acting as if they do not think the primary purpose of their business is to make money. They're so intent on developing their own personal projects, they forget the importance of keeping expenditures at rock bottom.

Let's be fair. I admit that, in their own minds, such executives honestly believe their pet projects will eventually benefit the firm. But at what price?

If the business goes broke, or if profit is too meager to properly finance expansion, then all their work will have gone for nothing. It happens that way, sometimes.

Here's an example:

Too Big Too Fast

I knew an experienced business consultant who was made president of a small company. The firm's annual volume was less than $1,000,000. The new president, who had done good work for some really big outfits (as a consultant), began to organize the firm along "big company" lines.

High-salaried executives were put on the payroll . . . in jobs set up along perfectly sound management lines. The new organization chart was something any *large* company could be proud of. But it did not fit the needs of that company at that time.

Departments were set up to look after matters which previously no one had had time to supervise. More people were hired. All principles of good management were put into effect — except one: *the new president seemed to forget that all these things had to be paid for out of profits.*

There was no surplus, no reserve worth mentioning . . . not enough profit to support these new functions and functionaries.

Soon the company was in serious financial trouble. Profits were virtually wiped out. Banks would not lend the firm any working capital. Except for fast action by the board of directors, who removed the president from office, the company would have gone under. Even then, it took a strong and sustained economy program to put the firm back on its feet.

Spending Reduces Profit, Always

In ancient Egypt, Pharoah once got the idea that the Israelites could be forced to make bricks without straw — a prime ingredient in bricks of that day. This was an obvious absurdity to Moses, who was sufficiently familiar with the brick-making processes of the period to know that you just can't make anything without having some raw materials to start with.

Some modern business leaders seem to think like the old Pharaoh. They seem to think you can take profit out of a business without putting very much into it. They don't seem to recognize one of the rudiments of successful management: *the first function of any business is to stay in business, and you cannot stay in business very long without profit.*

Efficient management cuts costs on everything going into the business — as much as practicably possible. This sort of cost-cutting applies to materials, time, and every other item of expense. The successful management man, and the young executive who's on his way to the top, watches every expense item. He's always on the lookout for ways to reduce cost without impairing efficiency. He is cost-conscious in everything he does and thinks about.

S-P-E-N-D-I-N-G Does Not Spell SUCCESS

There's a very simple formula; you've no doubt seen it:

Income $1.00; outlay $1.01.................Bankruptcy
Income $1.00; outlay $0.99.................Success

Two cents is the difference between success and failure, by that formula. In a business handling millions of dollars, such as a supermarket chain, for instance, a difference of 2¢ on the dollar will often spell the difference between dividend or no dividend, profit or loss, success or failure. "Look out for the pennies and the dollars will take care of themselves" is just as good advice today as it was centuries ago when some unrecorded sage uttered the famous words.

Every business, sooner or later, stands or falls by that simple formula. It's so simple, so elementary, that it's easily overlooked . . . and there's a tendency to overlook it in an expanding organization, especially in this day of distorted values due to tremendous Government spending.

You can't spend your way to success, but saving will surely get you there. This is true of companies as well as of individuals.

I have seen a giant firm become more interested in the share of the market held by one of its items than in the profit or loss shown by that product. One of my first jobs was in marketing research. I've listened to executives gloat over the fact that a certain product had gained one or two percentage points in share of market over a leading competitor. Not one word was said about the half-million-dollar advertising outlay it took to achieve this small increase. Those men did not care that they spent two dollars in selling expense for every dollar of increased sales (which amounted to a few pennies of increased profit). Fortunately, that situation was soon changed by top management.

Maybe you've heard the Successful Man described as "one who earns more than his wife can spend"; and the Successful Woman as "one who finds such a man."* If there's a man in business who thinks he can stay in business very long without earning more than he spends . . . he's not a successful business man; he's either a plain fool or a con man in the championship class.

Invest For Tomorrow, Sure . . . But Don't Over-invest

Many times it is necessary to spend money today for results expected in the distant future. But, such investment spending must be well conceived and basically sound. Too often, money is spent merely to reach a goal without studying to see whether that goal will pay out sufficient profit once it is reached.

Nearly every executive is vulnerable to the kind of thinking that can result in expenditure of company money for projects that can never pay a profit. You believe in your ideas, just as I believe

---

*Quoted in *Speaker's Encyclopedia* (ed. Jacob M. Braude; Prentice-Hall, Inc., 1957).

in mine. You believe, and believe strongly, that your ideas will benefit your company. That's natural.

Early in my career, I spent a bit of money that never turned a profit for my company. Yet, at the time, I *knew* it was a good investment.

I was in charge of Research and Development for a medium-size company. My primary duties were in product development. Because I had a background in market research, I felt strongly that we needed a statistician to keep track of sales trends within a sample of typical outlets. I set up an elaborate system for recording movement of individual products in each of the control stores.

For three months, my statistician accumulated data religiously. She recorded the ups and downs of demand by product groups and in total. I thought to myself, "Won't we be glad that we have this data two years from now, when it will be necesssary to review our sales policies."

But the company was not making much money. Management decreed that every department's budget must be cut, and quick. This was the least necessary of all functions in my department, so I agreed to cut it out. To my surprise, every department head had some pet project, just as important to him as this one was to me. When they were all dropped, we started showing a healthy profit.

Suddenly, I realized that I had not seen any possible value to the company of these other "pet projects" in other departments. Then I realized how foolish I had been. My own pet statistical project, no doubt, had seemed just as unnecessary to those other department heads.

Finally, I came to understand a fact which I believe is basic: *A particular program is good or bad depending on the company's ability to finance it and still show an adequate profit.* What is gained by accumulating reams of data for future reference if the cost pushes the company into bankruptcy?

So, be sure a project is vital before you recommend spending money, or very much time. Even then, don't go overboard. Don't let your enthusiasm for a certain project affect your good, hard-headed business judgment.

Many Ways To Keep Costs Down

Also, keep expenditures for vital functions to an absolute mini-mum. There are, usually, many ways to do this.

Perhaps you can find a new way to do the same job, as a by-product of another necessary function. With a little reorganization you may be able to save thousands of dollars each year. That would be a direct contribution to net profit. Such savings often contribute more to net profit (and faster) than do many times the same dollar amount in sales increases. The old adage "a penny saved is a penny earned" was never truer than in today's overhead-heavy corporate enterprises.

Sometimes you can find ways to save money for your company by introducing an entirely new concept, a new way of thinking. For example, a company distributed its products through three major channels: route sales, direct shipments, and sales through wholesalers. A test study was made on route sales, subdivided by class of trade and by size of customer. The study showed that 87 percent of route customers were probably handled at a loss. Closer study of other channels of distribution led to revamping of the firm's entire distribution system. Profits shot up, of course.

In another case, a cost analysis showed industrial users (sold direct) to be more profitable customers than were dealers. However, variations in cost and profit by size of customer were more significant than variations by channels of distribution. Salesmen were told to stop calling on small dealers. They began spending more time with large industrial accounts. Distribution costs were cut 38 percent in one year. Cuts like that can make the profit picture a lot prettier.

What About Your Department?

Are these extreme examples? I think not.

Could similar results be achieved right in your own department? Probably, I daresay.

Spectacular results have been achieved by thousands of corporations when they converted to "scientific management." Of course, skepticism greeted the reports and proponents of such "new-fangled ideas" as time-and-motion studies and cost-accounting when they came on the business scene.

Around the turn of the century, Frederick Taylor developed certain principles of scientific production management. Great achievements have been made in increased output per man-hour and in reduced unit factory costs, through application of those principles. Today, hardly any forward-looking business person questions those great achievements.

Yet, almost any hard-headed, cold-eyed production man will readily admit that unit production costs are still very far from an irreducible minimum. Don't be surprised, therefore, to find places where striking achievements in cost-cutting can be made in your company, or in your own department. Look for them. The successful, progressive executive never stops looking for opportunities to cut costs without hurting production and profit.

Know Your Budget

There's much misdirected effort, even in the more efficiently-managed companies. Consequently, there are many important opportunities for reducing costs. One sure way to reduce costs in your own area of responsibility is to start out by getting a thorough knowledge of your firm's budgetary policies and procedures. If you know what goes into making up your budget, and if you are sure you understand what your company is trying to accomplish, it will be easier for you to make a genuine contribution to reduction in operating costs.

Budgeting is simply a management tool used to plan, carry out, and control the operations of a business. It establishes predetermined objectives and provides the basis for measuring performance against these objectives. Stripped of its mystery, this is just another way of saying it is "business planning." Budgeting should not be regarded as just "a way to worry about your money before you spend it instead of afterwards," as an after-dinner speaker once said.

There are many kinds of budgets — the advertising budget, the research budget, the direct labor budget, the material and production budget, the cash budget, the master budget, and the summary budget, such as the balance sheet and profit-and-loss budget.

Somewhere among these budgets are some estimates of what you will probably be authorized to spend to carry out the assignments of management. By setting up this budget in advance, management is provided with a means to plan the most economical use of labor, material, and other expense. It also provides for control of funds spent, thereby preventing waste if spending is done intelligently.

Stay "On Top" Of Your Budget

Usually, a department head will be consulted when the budget is being prepared. Then he actually has a hand in determining the amount it is estimated his department will spend during the ensuing period. All too often, however, this preliminary discussion with the budget director or a member of his staff is the last time a department head will refer to the budget. Only if expenditures get entirely out of hand will management call him in and ask for an explanation. Otherwise, the very existence of the budget will probably be forgotten for another year.

That does not happen, in the case of the alert young executive who's on his way up to the presidency . . . and that's you, of course. You'll know your budget, inside and out, and you'll do your best to "stay on top" of your budget and within it at the same time.

In watching your budget, remember that if you spend too little and do not get the required results, then you are not fulfilling your obligations to your firm. If, on the other hand, you get an idea which cannot help having a quick payout in profit, but the cost exceeds your budget, then it will pay you to have a working knowledge of what went into the budget figures. Then, you can either reduce outlay on a less vital function, or sell management on upping your budget to take care of this special project. In either case, you are better armed if you have a thorough knowledge of budgetary policies and how they affect your department.

To Summarize

Money is one of your main tools. Budget it carefully. Cultivate a mind for figures. Always think like a controller, or treasurer. Look at everything with the eyes of a cost-accountant.

Sound planning is preliminary and necessary to sound progress. When you get to the top, you'll be doing a lot of long-range planning. Planning is impossible without an understanding of and use of budgetary principles. Planning, thinking, and working in line with sound budgetary practices will help speed you to the top of the firm before you're forty.

11

BE NICE TO YOUR BOSS —
EVEN NICER TO YOUR SUBORDINATES

A good administrator is liked and respected by his subordinates. If the boss is known, behind his back, as Terrible Tom, Do-It-Quick Dick, or Horrible Harry, there's a fair chance he will not be going much higher up the executive ladder . . . because *his subordinates will not be pushing him up.*

Running a business is a far cry from a popularity contest. There's no question, though, that employees will work harder and more effectively if they feel confidence in and enthusiasm for their boss.

Wages And Hours Get Undue Attention

Poor pay and long hours are not the major causes of industrial unrest . . . believe it or not. The notion that they are is unsound, both psychologically and statistically.

Wages-and-hours disputes get undue prominence in press reports of industrial conflict. They're convenient hooks to hang stories on . . . that's probably the main reason. It's only natural, then, that workers themselves would consider wages and hours as the major causes of employee unrest. Many employees are emotionally and intellectually inarticulate. In other words, *workers don't think —* very thoroughly, very deeply . . . as a rule. They have vague, unanalyzed discontents. They know something is wrong, but they don't know quite what it is. It's *easy* to conclude that something's wrong with management — something they can't do much about. That's just the way human nature works.

Wages and hours are definite, objective things. They're easily understood, even by the less intelligent. Therefore, employee discontent most often takes the external form of demands for shorter hours and higher wages.

Here Comes Psychology

The enlightened executive knows that although part of labor unrest comes from economic factors, there is also an important psychological side. Employees show signs of low morale when their work does not give the personal, inner satisfactions every human being requires.

The enlightened executive can fill the hunger for satisfaction by praising employees when they do a good job. He must have an understanding of the employee as an individual.

There has been, and still is, a lack of understanding of the employee as an individual, even by executives who have come up from the very bottom ranks. This lack of understanding is brought out clearly by a study reported by Fosdick to the 1939 Convention of the National Retail Dry Goods Association.*

Several hundred employers and 3,000 employees scattered throughout the U. S. were asked to rate the importance of eight morale factors. The results are summarized in the following table:

RANK ASSIGNED VARIOUS FACTORS OF MORALE
BY EMPLOYEES AND EMPLOYERS

MORALE ITEM	EMPLOYEE RANKING	EMPLOYER RANKING
Credit for all work done	1	7
Interesting Work	2	3
Fair Pay	3	1
Understanding and Appreciation	4	5
Counsel on Personal Problems	5	8
Promotion on Merit	6	4
Good Physical Working Conditions	7	6
Job Security	8	2

Notice that the employees as a group considered *Credit for Work Done* to be of paramount importance, whereas the employers put it seventh in the group of eight items.

On the other hand, the employers assigned the next-to-top rank to job security, while the employee put it eighth.

This study strongly suggests that the employer has frequently

*Hartman, G. C. and Newcomb, T. (Ed.): *Industrial Conflict, A Psychological Interpretation* (The Cordon Co., 1943, pp. 118-19).

been out of touch with the real problems and aspirations of his employees. The notion that money paid as salaries or wages is the common denominator for all human aspirations is no longer accepted by students of human nature.

Importance Of Human Relations Now Recognized

Fortunately, with the growth of Industrial Relations Departments within the larger manufacturing firms, many business leaders are recognizing the importance of human relations in administering their companies.

Recently I sat in on a meeting of plant managers of one of the world's largest drug manufacturers. The chairman of the board was addressing the group on the importance of good worker relations. He had just returned from a tour of the firm's plants in Europe, where the rate of production per worker was far lower than in the United States. The European plants, he pointed out, have enough volume to utilize the same degree of mechanization as the U. S. plants have. Why was European output lower?

In the opinion of this enlightened business leader, output was lower in Europe because the European attitude toward the worker was entirely different from the American attitude.

He recounted an instance of walking into an office where several employees were attending a meeting. His host, the plant manager, made it a point to introduce him (the chairman of the board) to those at the management level, but he ignored those with jobs lower than supervisory.

How can a worker be expected to harbor less than resentment toward management when he is treated as an inferior?

Every effective leader of men understands these basic human motivations. And, understanding them, his attitude and actions are accordingly governed.

Business Leaders Quoted

Praise is better than blame, and every man works for self-and social-approval.

Charles M. Schwab, famed head of U. S. Steel, then Bethlehem Steel, once said: "There is nothing that so kills the ambition of a man as adverse criticism from his superior. If a man does a good job, I do not hesitate to tell him so. . . . A little bit of praise affects the sweating puddler as it does the President of the United States."

Andrew Carnegie was Charles M. Schwab's boss. He clearly recognized the great importance of human relations in business. When asked whether he could not have Mr. Schwab's services for less money than Schwab was getting, Carnegie replied: "I am in business to make men as well as to make money."

Eli Lily, founder of the pharmaceutical house bearing his name, said: "The first responsibility of our supervisors is to build men and women, then medicine."

Henry Ford, II, has said: "If we can solve the problems of human relations in industrial production, I believe we can make as much progress toward lower costs during the next ten years as we made during the past quarter-century through the development of the machinery of mass production."

Harry A. Bullis, the Iowa bookkeeper who became Chairman of the Board at General Mills, has predicted: "The second half of our century will be marked by inspiring progress in the field of human relations."

Dr. Hurlock's Experiment

Some years ago an experiment was conducted by Dr. Elizabeth B. Hurlock to compare the relative effectiveness of *praise* and *reproof*. The test was conducted on students, but there seems no good reason why the generalizations which resulted should not be extended to include working adults.

Dr. Hurlock set up four groups of students, to determine whether *praise* or *reproof* would more effectively stimulate them to solve arithmetic problems faster. Thirty problems were to be solved in fifteen minutes. The experiment lasted five days. Previous work had shown all the problems equally difficult for all the students.

The first day, all four groups solved an average of 11.8 problems in the time allowed.

In order to have complete control in the experiment, Dr. Hurlock not only had a *praised* and a *reproved* group, but she also set up a group that heard the praise and reproof directed to others, but they themselves were entirely ignored. Finally, she included a control group who heard neither praise nor reproof administered to the others.

Results for the four groups are shown in Figure 1, Page 78. The control group serves as a standard against which the effects of the other conditions can be judged. The general trend for the control group is slightly downward.

All three of the special motivating conditions give rise to more production. Even the ignored group shows some improvement, but it becomes progressively less as the experiment continues.

On the second day, there is little to choose between *praise* and *reproof;* but after that the *reproved* group steadily loses its initial gain. The trend for the *praised* group, on the other hand, is entirely different; throughout the five-day period, it continues to improve. We must conclude, then, that *praise is much more effective as a motivating agent than is reproof.**

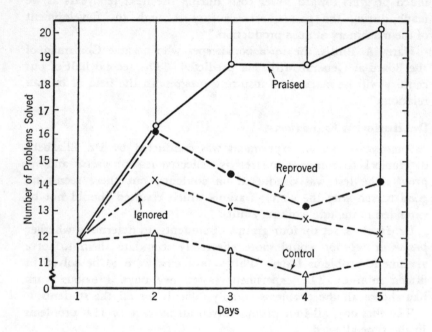

Why Treat Subordinates Better Than Superiors?

Being a warm-blooded human being, you may well ask: Why is it more important to be nice to subordinates than it is to be nice to superiors? Shouldn't I be nice to everybody?

Yes . . . up to a point.

But, don't overlook your ultimate goal . . . and don't overlook the essential steps leading toward that goal. Don't forget that subordinates and superiors are two different categories of people.

*Valentine, Willard L.: *Experimental Foundations of General Psychology* (Ed.: 1946, pp. 198-201).

First, let's consider your subordinates. Your superiors judge you on results, remember. If you get results by generously passing out praise (to your subordinates), then it stands to reason that this is the thing to do. By all means! And by every way you can figure to do it . . . within the limits of reasonableness and good taste.

What about superiors? Naturally, you'll be courteous to them, just as to everybody else. After all, they are human beings too. However, there will be times when you will be forced to fight for a program in which you believe. Those men at the top level are strong-willed. Often, they'll say "No" to a project on the first reading, on general principles. One wise executive I know has a favorite saying on this subject: "It's always easier to say 'No.' Whenever you say 'Yes,' wheels start turning . . . and there's no telling what can come of it."

Don't Let Questions Frighten You

Many top-level administrators make it a habit to question everything. It's their way of finding out whether you believe in a program yourself.

When I was doing market research work for a large soap company some years ago we had a vice president for advertising who practiced this technique continually.

One day my partner and I presented a plan for an advertising sales test. We had spent days and days selecting the best test markets, and we felt certain we had everything covered for a maximum reading of results. After glancing over the proposal for a few minutes, the vice president turned to me and said: "Can't you do better than that? Take this back and study it over. When you have a good sales test worked out, come back and see me."

In a couple of days we were back in his office explaining that we had gone over the entire test, and that we were convinced that it had been set up along sound lines. Without a further word, he grasped the write-up and penned his initials and a big "O.K." He was just testing us to see whether we had really thought the thing through and would stand by our convictions.

You Must Be Persistent, Sometimes

Then, there is always room for an honest difference of opinion among executives. In every firm, thousands of decisions must be made each year. The vast majority of them could go either way without seriously disrupting the company's operations. It is quite difficult, sometimes, to decide which viewpoint is the correct one . . . if, indeed, there is a correct one. Few business problems have as clear-cut answers as problems in arithmetic.

Because of this, it is important for the young executive to be articulate in defense of the policies about which he has deep convictions. He must be able to show his associates that his plan *could be* the *best* answer, even though it may not be the *only* answer. He should never be discourteous, but he must be persistent in his quest for a favorable decision from the men who have the power to make such a decision.

This is why some committee meetings in big companies can get more than a little "hot" at times. When you get a group of men with strong personalities together in a room, there is bound to be a rise of temperatures as the discussion progresses.

Speak Up

While you are in the stage of promoting an idea, you should use every technique at your command to create a favorable impression. Invariably, you will have to answer charges that infer you have not thought out your program. You cannot afford to let such charges go unanswered.

This is the time for strength. Speak out. Do not be afraid to defend your ideas, and your thoroughness in developing your ideas. Your superiors will respect you for it, and you will have a better chance to make a genuine contribution to your company's progress.

Finally, a word of caution. If you are unsuccessful in convincing management that your idea should be tried, do not harbor any resentment. File your idea. It may just fit another situation, later.

Sometimes there are economic reasons behind a decision to shelve a seemingly good idea. And, sometimes, you are not in a position to understand and appreciate all the reasons. If you sulk or continue to needle your superiors after it becomes obvious that your program is impossible to put into effect, then you'll soon gain for yourself the reputation of a "non-team" man.

Don't Encourage Ulcers

Drs. Donald and Eleanor Laird have some pertinent thoughts on this matter of sulking and resentment:

> Resentment is a factor in causing ulcers, but a different kind of resentment than in high blood pressure. Blood-pressure resentment is toward being bossed; ulcer resentment is toward the world in general for not letting the individual be more of a

success . . . His underlying sourness against the world in general sours his stomach. The pills for sour stomach do not change the sour attitudes. After an emotional upset, the sour stomach may begin to digest itself in one place. That is the start of the ulcer . . .

Ulcers need not be a price paid for success. But they are part of the price when a man tries to achieve success in the ulcer way . . . After medical care has cured an ulcer, another may be formed if the person persists in his ulcer personality.

Success does not cure the ulcer personality. The man needs the things he unconsciously hopes success will bring — affection and approval. The boss who never says a good word, who keeps employees guessing about whether or not they are approved, adds to their ulcer attitude.*

To Summarize

So, in your quest for recognition within the management team, make it easy on yourself and your subordinates by recognizing them as human beings with the desire to be recognized for their value. If you are nice to them, they will be nice to you by pushing out more and more production.

Bosses, too, are human. They crave appreciation. But, if your boss resists a program in which you believe strongly, don't be afraid to stand up and be counted . . . you *will* be counted, standing up, before your name is on the door marked "President."

---

*Laird, Donald A. and Eleanor C.: *Practical Business Psychology* (McGraw-Hill, 1956, p. 336).

12

YOU MUST COMMUNICATE —

If You Anticipate Becoming President

"Why do you make your directives sound so strong?" I once asked a high-ranking executive.

"This message must go through five men before it gets down to the people who will have to carry it out," he answered. "If I do not say precisely what I mean, and in language that cannot be misinterpreted, it is an absolute certainty that the communication will be watered down to the point where I myself would not recognize it."

My friend was describing one of the most perplexing problems facing corporation managements today . . . the problem of *communications.*

Too Much Secrecy

If you want to qualify for a corporate presidency some day in the future, you might just as well start learning to cope with this problem right now. As a matter of fact, if you do not recognize the importance of perfecting your communicating techniques, you may never get within reaching distance of the top.

For one thing, too many department heads, and certainly too many company managements, employ too much secrecy in running the business. Sometimes this secrecy serves only to enhance the individual's opinion of his own importance (because he knows things he can't tell to just everybody), and simultaneously to widen the gulf between management and managed.

Words From Wise Men

Charles R. Hook, Chairman of American Rolling Mills Company (Armco Steel), once recommended as a slogan for modern management: *Take the mystery out of business.*

Admiral Ben Moreel, head of Jones & Laughlin Steel Corporation, suggested eliminating the so-called "management secrets." Let every member of the team (and your team may be a department or a section) know what's being planned, what's in the works . . . at least a general idea and the general direction.

James G. Shennan, President of Elgin National Watch Company, made a good point when he said: "You cannot have an efficient organization unless it is an informed organization."

M. M. Olander, Director of Industrial Relations for Owens-Illinois Glass Company, made this statement in a speech before the West Virginia Manufacturers' Association:

"The good supervisor tries to avoid or eliminate situations which unnecessarily create frustration or anger. He does this by keeping his eye out for the many petty annoyances that arouse people's anger . . . by keeping people *INFORMED instead of uneasy.*"

Communication Techniques

What are some of the techniques of communicating?

The principle methods are:

1. *The Written Word.* In the complex organizations of present-day business, it is inevitable that a considerable portion of all communicating is done through writing. Sales memos, policy memos, letters, bulletins, directives, manuals . . . these are all effective tools for communicating through the written word.

2. *The Spoken Word.* Thousands of day-to-day instructions must be passed along to subordinates verbally. While the spoken word is essential to the proper operation of a business, it is also the most vulnerable to misunderstanding. Many important projects have bogged down simply because someone did not make himself clear or because someone else did not listen carefully.

3. *The Pictured Idea.* Confucius said "One picture is worth ten thousand words." Modern business endorses this old Chinese axiom by wide use of illustrated posters, slide films, motion pictures, and other illustrated methods and media in employee relations as well as in public relations.

Don't Be MIS-understood

Even when communications are handled in a competent manner, it is possible for policies to be misunderstood.

A man of mature business experience once told me: "It is important to make yourself understood, but it is even more important to be sure you will not be *mis*understood." A fine point, there . . . but useful.

A supply clerk for a motor freight line turned down a requisition from the repair shop for a fuel pump. The repair foreman who made the request knew there should be one in stock, and he asked the clerk why he did not send it.

"Yes, I have one," replied the clerk, "but it's the only one I have and the manual says I am to keep one on hand at all times. If I give it to you, I would not have *any* on hand."

If the clerk's boss had spent a little more time with the clerk, explaining the *reasoning* behind this policy, he surely would not have made a silly blunder like that. He needed to be *oriented* on how things are supposed to run in the shop. He needed to know that it was his job to furnish parts and not to "keep them in inventory." Here was a perfect example of communications that had broken down.

How Can You Develop A Good System Of Communications?

There is no simple answer, of course. Here are a few tools that have proved helpful in communicating with employees:

1. *Clearly-stated Policy Statements.* Top management should develop its policies with exactitude and reduce them to writing that is crystal clear . . . not just written so they can be understood, but written in such a way that they cannot be *mis*understood. Then these statements, sometimes in *policy manual* form, should be distributed to all levels of supervision and each supervisor should be trained in applying them.

2. *Simply-worded Employee Manuals.* While the Policy Statement, often, is phrased in quasi-legal language, the wording essential to employee understanding should be an informal, easy-to-absorb document, written from the employee's rather than the company's viewpoint.

3. *Bulletin Board Notices.* A favorite way for executives to talk to lower-level employees is through bulletin board notices. Some firms make such announcements sound like board of directors resolutions. Such formal notices often make workers feel regimented, which is not good. A clear, friendly notice with a per-

sonal touch helps employees feel there must be a "real guy" upstairs in the office, rather than a legal automaton.

Bulletin board notices need not be limited to layoffs, new schedules, holidays, and other routine matters. Many workers like to see that their company is making progress in such things as new product development, sales, earnings, and other matters that are vital to their future. Some of the publicity that appears in newspapers should first appear on the bulletin board, so that employees learn of them at the plant, not from friends or news articles.

4. *Posters.* Another popular medium is the poster. While this is an excellent means of improving morale and plugging certain projects such as safety campaigns, it cannot be substituted for other methods of communication.

5. *Special Memos Or Letters To Employees.* When a top executive is especially anxious to get a point across, or stress a certain policy or plan, he can use the medium of personal memos or letters. This means of communicating has the advantage of appearing, and indeed it is, more personal than most of the others. Some firms have introduced special annual reports to employees similar in form to the traditional Stockholders' Report. It takes time and imagination to prepare such a report because, to get the maximum effect, it is important to avoid "talking down" to the employee.

6. *Employee Publications.* Employee publications serve a useful function in keeping personnel informed on the aims and progress of the company. It lends interest and dignity to a person's job to hear about such things as employee recreation, promotions, suggestions and what was done about them, awards the company has won, and contributions the company has made to the community and the nation.

7. *Loud-speaker Systems.* Sometimes an executive will choose to talk with large groups at one time by means of a loud-speaker system. This has been done successfully by many industries to transmit the dynamic personality of the chief executive or other supervisory personnel to the men and women at their desks and machines.

8. *Personal Interviews.* I know a department store president who made it a habit to have a personal chat with every member

of his entire company, from vice president to truck driver, at least once each quarter. "This is how I learn what's going on in the businesss," he once told me.

In very large corporations, it is impossible for the chief executive to speak personally with every employee in the organization. But a certain amount of face-to-face communication is essential to keeping both *managed* and *management* informed.

Here's a true story bearing on this point:

Soon after Sidney L. Willson became President of American Writing Paper Company he began touring the company's plants. On one such visit, he got away from escorting officials and engaged a veteran workman in conversation.

"How long have you been here?" asked the new president, not identifying himself.

"Twenty-three years."

"I've been with the Company only a few weeks," said Willson. "There are a lot of things I don't know yet. Tell me about your job."

The old-timer launched into a detailed description of the paper-making process, including his ideas about some ways it could be improved. It was the first time in twenty-three years that his ideas had been solicited. At the end of the conversation, he asked Willson what his job was.

"I'm supposed to help everybody," replied Willson. "Sometimes I help the auditor and sometimes I help the office boy. If I can't help you and the other fellows here in the mill, I'll be falling down on my job . . . I'm the president."

Goal: Understanding

No matter what medium of communication is used, it should not be limited to messages of exhortation or rosy reports of achievements. Channels of communication should be used primarily to enable the company's top management and its rank-and-file employees to understand each other better, not merely to overwhelm with propaganda. No channel of communication is effective unless it has prestige in the mind of the employee.

Channels of communication must be established, kept open, and used . . . consistently and wisely. But if an executive should develop the impression that these channels can be a synthetic substitute for a genuine interest in employee relations, he will one day suddenly and painfully realize his error.*

To Summarize

Let the team know what's cooking. They'll work harder to enjoy it.

Information prevents frustration. Keep employees informed on matters affecting their jobs and their future.

Speak and write so clearly that you cannot be *mis*understood.

Always speak and write like a human being.

Remember Sidney L. Willson's philosophy: *the president's job is to help everybody*. Start doing it now.

You must communicate if you anticipate becoming president before you're forty.

---

*Adapted from J. K. Lasser: *Business Management Handbook* (McGraw-Hill, 1952, pp. 342-47, *passim*).

13

HAVE THE COURAGE TO BE WRONG

QUESTION: True or False? *The way to get to the top in business is to avoid making mistakes.*
ANSWER: False.

In politics, as in surgery, a big mistake can be fatal. But, in a fast-moving, modern corporation, mistakes are inevitable. It's the number and frequency that makes differences on balance sheets.

If you're working as a corporation executive must work, you can't be right all the time. Keep on trying . . . but in the back of your mind save a little space to remember that you, too, can make mistakes . . . and you will.

Don't let mistakes throw you. A mistake should be a teacher . . . not a stumbling-block. The only way you can be defeated by your mistakes alone is to fail to correct them.

"Experience is a great thing," somebody once said; "it helps us recognize our mistakes the second time around." And the village wit is reported to have remarked: "The only people in our town who never make mistakes are those resting over yonder in the graveyard." Theodore Roosevelt said: "Show me a man who makes no mistakes and I will show you a man who doesn't do things." You've probably heard that a bachelor is a man who has never made the same mistake once.

Don't Be Timid

Don't be overly cautious about avoiding errors in judgment . . . the first time, anyway. The timid man deprives himself of a lot of experience and stands to miss out on a lot of life's great satisfactions . . . whether we're talking about marriage, mambo, or commerce.

Don't be so conscious of the possibility of error that you fail to exercise judgment. Don't be paralyzed by apprehension. If that sort of thing becomes a habit, you can defeat yourself. You can do it in either of two ways:

(1) *You will hesitate to make decisions.* That means you will not be fulfilling your executive responsibilities.

(2) *You will spend a lot of time defending your decisions, even after you, yourself, know they are wrong.*

Either of these weaknesses can be fatal to a man with presidential aspirations. Watch out for them. Don't let them trip you. As U. S. Presidential candidate Adlai E. Stevenson once facetiously suggested, you should not "try to climb the ladder of success wrong by wrong."

Hesitation, Vacillation . . . Then Frustration

Let's explore, for a moment, the first shortcoming — *hesitating to make decisions.*

The executive's main job is to make decisions. You are supposed to have the background of training and experience necessary to lead subordinates and to help them solve their problems. This means making decisions . . . every day, every hour.

Once I had to remind an office manager that he would have no job unless there were problems. He was complaining about the great number of times he was interrupted every day to answer questions from his clerks. He considered necessary decision-making as an interruption to his otherwise smooth routine. He just didn't see decision-making as a vital part of his job.

Decision-making *is* vital. If there were no decisions to be made, the executive might as well never come to the office . . . and the company might as well save his salary. If everything ran smoothly, and a firm could depend on its clerks to carry out every assignment, the need for supervisory people would be eliminated. Of course, the next logical step after eliminating need is to eliminate cost.

But no successful business runs without supervision. Problems are coming up, all the time. Decisions must be made. Plans must be laid for solving tomorrow's problems. All this requires men and women capable of meeting these challenges day-by-day, with the courage to make decisions.

And the courage to make decisions means also the courage to be wrong, now and then.

Indecision Kills Volition

If you are so afraid of possible errors that you fail to make decisions, it will be just a matter of time before your department bogs down in a quagmire of inactivity. Far better to make an occasional wrong decision than to deprive your subordinates of direction and guidance in their work.

Suppose you do make a wrong decision. Soon it will be obvious to nearly everybody. Then, a quick reversal is usually possible . . . before your face gets too red. But if no decision is made, there is no way of knowing the correct answer to that problem.

A high official of one of the nation's leading sales organizations was being considered for the presidency. One of the board members pointed out that this individual's major experience had been in research work, where his talents for painstaking analysis were both necessary and beneficial. But, pointed out this board member, this same painstaking approach to a problem, so essential in research, could be a hindrance to a top corporation officer. It could slow down his decision-making.

Before deciding between this man and other candidates, the board of directors decided to give all candidates a scientifically-designed test for measuring executive capabilities. Results were most interesting. The research man showed up as excellently qualified for research and development, but poorly qualified for a top executive position like president. He simply could not make decisions fast enough. True, he would make fewer mistakes than average; but, at the top, the premium is on speedy decisions with a high average of correctness, rather than fewer decisions with absolute accuracy.

Don't Worry

Philip D. Wagoner became president of General Vehicles Company, a General Electric subsidiary, at 34. Later he was named head of Underwood-Elliott-Fisher. The office machines firm later changed to Underwood Corporation. In his first presidential post, Wagoner learned a valuable lesson about mistakes. Here's how he spoke of that experience, some years later:

> I immediately found (as soon as I became president) that one of the things I had to do was to make important decisions. I

was a little confused as to whether my decisions would turn out right or wrong. I made up my mind I would watch the results of each decision and if it was not right, I would change it. I began to worry more and more. In two weeks I was watching so many decisions and their results that I did not have time to make new ones. I was in trouble. I took off a few days and went fishing. On that fishing trip I made up my mind I would not worry. And ever since that time I have refused to worry over decisions. Like everyone else, I have had a normal number of problems in my business life, but by failing to worry I have never had difficulty in getting a good night's sleep and waking refreshed for the problems of the next day.*

Worrying over mistakes and consequences of your decisions can bring on ulcers and other unwelcome conditions, about as quickly as anything. Do your best, then entertain no regrets about what you've done . . . but of course, if your best of today needs correcting tomorrow, correct it. You should recognize that there are some things you cannot do; probably nobody could.

Fretting and fuming over things you cannot accomplish can injure your mental and physical health. Worry invites trouble . . . and you'll have enough of that without sending out invitations. George Washington Lyon described worry as "the interest paid by those who borrow trouble." Learn how to get along without borrowing trouble, and you won't have to pay the interest.

Without Mistakes, You'll Never Learn

Unless you're different from other human beings, you do not and will not learn very much nor very thoroughly without making a few mistakes in the process. If you're like the rest of us, you did not learn to add or subtract without being corrected now and then. You didn't learn to read without mispronouncing a few words. You didn't learn to write without occasional misspelling.

You'll have to keep on learning if you're to keep on climbing. So make up your mind to keep on learning and to keep on climbing, in spite of mistakes you're bound to make.

I have heard more than one scientist say he never made a discovery without making some mistakes first. Trial and error, test and try, check and prove — that's the way to certainty in science. The way to success in business is by a parallel path.

Big men in business know this. They don't forget all their own mistakes. They know you'll be making some of your own.

---

*Quoted in B. C. Forbes: *101 Unusual Experiences* (B. C. Forbes & Sons, 1952).

When I was living in Miami, soon after World War II, the Keyes Company was rated as Florida's No. 1 real estate brokerage firm. Kenneth Keyes, Jr., son of the founder, was quite active in the business, while finding time to teach a course in the University of Miami's Business School, participate in civic activities, and to write a very helpful book, *How To Develop Your Thinking Ability* (published by McGraw-Hill in 1950).

In that book, Mr. Keyes says: "I have very little confidence in people who are not big enough to admit their mistakes. I have a sneaking suspicion that most of their ideas are simply mistakes they should have outgrown a long time ago."

Profit From Mistakes

Austin Inglehart, when he was top executive at General Foods, told of a mistake he made when he was 16. He had worked hard and saved $500. A fast-talker sold him on investing his entire savings in a gold mine. He lost every cent. But, said Mr. Inglehart, it turned out to be a real good investment: the experience taught him early to be a very careful buyer.

Floyd Odlum, head of huge Atlas Corporation (closed-end investment trust) is said to have made a $30,000 mistake early in his business career. He lost that much in a margin stock speculation, but (so I have heard) he has never since bought securities on margin. He profited from that experience (mistake) in subsequent dealings . . . dealings which put him in control of many, many millions.

Likewise, your early mistakes (experiences, or reverses) can be helpful . . . if you are resourceful enough to make them serve you.

The resourceful man is never broken by "bad breaks." He may be knocked down, time after time. But he knows that being down doesn't necessarily mean failure. He knows that *staying down* does inevitably close the door to success. "The greatest mistake," said Dr. Frank Crane, "is giving up."

Get Out Of The Jam

It's often possible to capitalize on your mistakes, as well as on bad breaks. I heard of one company which used this technique deliberately in its Collection and Credit Department. To accounts with long-past-due balances, statements were sent showing incorrect amounts due — amounts way too high. These "mistakes" brought calls in a hurry . . . calls which constituted acknowledgment of obligations due and thereby re-opened discussions, which led to collection of some accounts which, otherwise, might have been written off as bad debts. But, it took a little courage as well as imagination in the Credit Department to send out those "mistakes."

Misfortune (mistakes of fortune), as well as mistakes in judgment, can sometimes get you in a jam. Paul G. Hoffman, the automobile salesman who climbed to the presidency of Studebaker, once expressed his thoughts on this matter thus: "When you are in a jam you do something about it, if you're smart. If you're not smart, you stay in the jam."

Speaking of jams, here's a true story about bread:

During the latter part of the Depression, Margaret Rudkin, wife of a Wall Street man, was experimenting with whole-wheat bread, trying to feed her young son back to health. She developed a recipe that yielded a flavor appealing not only to the ailing youngster with the finicky appetite, but which also drew *oh's* and *ah's* from her neighbors. She left a few loaves with her corner grocer one day, hot from the oven. He asked for more every day. Soon, Pepperidge Farm Bread was going strong all across the United States . . . and it started because Mrs. Rudkin was in a jam — her sick son just wouldn't eat regular bread.

Try Again

Having the courage to be wrong includes the ability to get up and try again every time you're floored by a mistake or a bad break. And, you're almost certain to be floored once in a while.

Herman Perl, head of Charlex Realty Company (No. 1 seller of Florida real estate in 1959, and a big factor in land development and sales in several other states), has had a number of business failures . . . but in 1959 he headed 18 corporations, with sales of over $25,000,000. Perl's flops have not been as big as his successes, of course; and the underlying reason is that he has never let a failure "get him down." As soon as an enterprise ceases to hold considerable promise of success, he folds it up, takes his loss, and forgets it, while pursuing something with greater promise.

Herman Perl is apparently guided by the same attitude held by the world's strike-out champion in baseball. This determined player fanned out 1,300 times during his career — the world's record. But he kept on swinging, and he's remembered, not as the strike-out champ, but as the "Home-Run King," Babe Ruth.

His 851 homers came to 65 percent of his number of strike-outs . . . but to baseball fans he'll always be the Home-Run King.

In business, of course, it's highly desirable to have more successes than failures . . . but if your successes are impressive enough, all of your failures will be forgotten, like Babe Ruth's strike-outs.

Help The Other Fellow To Be Right

So, learn to profit from misfortune or from your own mistakes . . . and do your profit-taking as early as you can. But, also take the next logical step.

Not only will you have the courage to admit and correct your own mistakes . . . you'll also be ready, willing, and anxious to "help the other fellow to be right." Dr. William J. Reilly, outstanding practicing psychologist and founder of the National Institute for Straight Thinking, says this is one of the best ways to work with people and get people to do more and better work.

"Let's assume," says Dr. Reilly, "that you're right and the boss is wrong or selfish. Nevertheless, no matter what a man's position is in business, his most important job in human relations is to get the active support and sponsorship of his immediate superior."

This principle works every day in selling, as every experienced salesman knows. "Any good salesman," says Dr. Reilly, "will tell you that even if he's 100 percent right and the prospect is 100 percent wrong, this isn't enough to assure him of an order. 'Winning an argument and losing a sale' is so common that any salesman worthy of the name will readily agree that 'thinking with the prospect' and 'helping him to be right' is the first step toward more sales and more profits."*

Bruce Barton's Boss

In his witty little book titled *This Way Up,* Cy Frailey quotes Bruce Barton, famous author and advertising man (BBD&O):

> One day a matter came up about which I happened to have the facts. My boss disagreed and, though I put up a good argument, he somewhat abruptly overruled me . . . Next morning he called me at my room at the YMCA, while I was dressing. 'I have been thinking about our discussion of yesterday, and I just want you to know that you were right and I was wrong,' he said. Yes, that was my boss, with an income of over $100,000 a year, calling a $40 a week youngster to say 'I was wrong.'

---

*If you are interested in going farther along that line of thought, you can spend a profitable couple of hours reading Dr. Reilly's book, *Successful Human Relations,* published by Harper & Bros. in 1952.

He had been 100 percent with me; after that he was the biggest man in town. Years have gone by . . . and it has interested me to observe how (men and women) divide into two classes: those who feel they have lowered themselves by admitting a mistake, and so try in every way to pass the buck, and those who come out in forth-right fashion and admit the facts. Almost always, the latter group make better members of an organization and go further up the ladder.

In the same handy, helpful little book, Cy Frailey gives his own nine-point definition of Big Men. The first one of these points: *Big men admit their own mistakes.**

Correction More Important Than Perfection

Some people mistakenly believe that a business requires of its executives something close to perfection in day-to-day decisions. Not so. I have heard executive after executive make the flat statement that he was satisfied if he averaged something more than 50 percent perfection in his decision-making.

Why is this true?

In nearly every business firm, hundreds of decisions are made daily. Most are minor, and a wrong judgment can have little effect on the company's long-range trend. Furthermore, a wrong decision can be corrected, usually within a matter of days or perhaps even hours.

Of course, there are a few big decisions every top executive must make from time to time. If they are the kind that can make or break a company, and if they cannot be reversed quickly with little harm to the firm, then it is advisable to take enough time to hear the *pros* and *cons* from all qualified subordinates before making a decision.

You'd be surprised, though, at how few decisions of this kind are made in a year in the average firm. If a great deal of money is involved, it is usually possible to test an idea on a limited scale to see whether it is practical. If not, the company is out very little, and no one can be critized for having a bad idea now and then. Just be careful not to make your *good* ideas conspicuous by their rarity.

Face It — You Can't Be Right Every Time

The second drawback can be even more serious than hesitation. Yes, *defending your own decisions too vehemently* can and will

---

*L. E. (Cy) Frailey: *This Way Up* (American Technical Society, 1946).

very quickly throw up a big roadblock in your path toward the presidency.

If you feel compelled to be correct in every one of your decisions, you will be naturally reluctant to admit you are wrong, ever. This will cause your superiors to think you are bull-headed and stubborn. They'll be right, no doubt. In addition, that kind of attitude postpones the day when corrective action can be taken.

The big sin in making a mistake is not recognizing it soon enough to correct a situation that has gone sour. Nothing is more pathetic than a man clinging to and defending his ideas after it is obvious to everyone else that his ideas are wrong.

Here's what happened a few years ago to a grocery chain buyer. He thought his job was to buy bread, bacon, and beans . . . and that was about all. He refused to recognize that the modern supermarket was expanding into products beyond the traditional food categories. He just would not buy non-food items, though competitor chains were expanding in that direction. It didn't take top management long to recognize this shortcoming. Our buyer friend still would not change his views. Management set up a separate non-foods buyer. Our friend had stopped growing . . . and in the world of business, when you stop growing, chances are you'll soon start *going* — in the opposite direction from up.

Men Can Learn From Mice

In a psychology book, I once read that *it's better to make 100 mistakes than to make just one mistake.* Reason: you then have 99 experiences where you probably will not make the same mistake again.

This is illustrated by the famous psychological experiment where a laboratory mouse is placed in a maze to see how quickly he can learn to find his way to the piece of cheese at the opposite end. First time around he gets into many blind alleys. He must turn back and try others. He does this over and over. Finally, he learns the correct route. After a few unsuccessful tries, he is able to find his way without mistakes, every time. It proves that he has learned by his mistakes. Most humans are smarter than mice . . . when they try.

Enlightened Companies Use This Principle

The same principle of *learning through mistakes* is used by enlightened firms, in management training programs for junior executives. They know that a man must have opportunities to exercise his own judgment. Therefore, they place him in positions where he will have to make decisions independent of his superiors. They know he will make some mistakes, but that he will learn in the process, thereby equipping him better for the big decisions he will make when he reaches a higher position in the company.

Ray Maher, one of the founders of Maher Management Company, owners of a dozen or more corporate enterprises, including many 7-Up bottling companies, once said to me: "When one of our plant managers makes an error of judgment, we do not rush to his rescue just as soon as we know about it. We like to have him stew in his juice for a while. It makes a better man out of him, and this is far more important than the little bit of money we lose during the interim."

To Summarize

Recognize that you cannot be correct in every decision, and that no one expects it of you. With that proper mental attitude, you'll be helping yourself up the ladder.

Adopt a positive policy. Make as many decisions as possible, as quickly as possible . . . using sound judgment, but without undue alarm if some decisions go sour.

When you do make an error in judgment, recognize it quickly and take immediate action to put things right.

You're always right when you have the courage to be wrong — and admit it, and correct it.

. . . That's another big step you must take, and take often, if you're going to be head of the firm before forty.

14

When Others' Brainwork Is Applied
YOUR BRAIN CAN BE MULTIPLIED

Persons close to one of the top corporation presidents in America know that he goes through a definite pattern each time an important decision is to be made.

He calls in a representative group of advisory experts from each division of the corporation. Some of them, he knows, will favor one view-point. Others, he believes, will lean in the opposite direction. He explains the problem at hand, thcn calls on each individual to give his opinion. During this period, the president says very little. He just sits back, soaking up the views of those he has asked to help him study the problem. Not until he has heard from every individual, every point of view, does he express his own opinion. Invariably, this president's own opinion has been influenced by the viewpoints of his advisors, the experts.

This is one of the techniques that made this corporation president successful. It enables him to accomplish two important objectives in dealing with men and with problems.

First, he found he could make a better decision if he listened to and considered all the possible viewpoints of the experts.

Second, he saw that the men under him would work together more smoothly if they knew their own opinions had been considered in making a decision.

What this corporation president was doing, in effect, was multiplying his own brain by using the minds and intellects of others.

It Can Make The Difference For You

This simple principle can be used in any business, very effectively. As a matter of fact, it can make the difference between a mediocre career and achieving your objective of a corporation presidency.

Give an I.Q. test to both senior and junior executives of any average American corporation, and you'll probably be surprised to find that the difference between the highest and lowest grade is much smaller than you had expected. Similarly, you would find not too close correlation between I.Q. and an executive's position in the company. You may very well find a research chemist hidden away in the depths of a laboratory who has an I.Q. of astronomical proportions, while the president or chairman of the board may show a grade considerably lower.

Bear in mind that I.Q. (Intelligence Quotient, a term developed by educational psychologists in the early 20th century) is not the only measure of a person's ability. It is a measure of the individual's *mental age* in relation to his chronological age. The person with a high I.Q. can usually do *most* things better (faster, more accurately, etc.) than the person with a lower I.Q. . . . but this does not mean that a high I.Q. is the sole passport to achievement, in business or anything else.

This explains, to some degree, why the chap who was voted "most likely to succeed" in business by his high school classmates sometimes lives out his day as assistant to the assistant bookkeeper; why a "nobody" in school sometimes becomes Mr. Moneybags a few years after graduation; why men like Lincoln, Franklin, and Edison have made great names for themselves without benefit of much formal education.

How, then, is a top corporation officer (even one with a relatively unimpressive I.Q.) able to rise to the top, and stay there? The answer, of course, involves many qualities which a chief executive must possess, beyond a high level of intelligence. One of these absolutely essential qualities is the *ability to use the brains of others.*

No matter how much knowledge a man may have about an enterprise, and no matter how keen his mind, he is still limited by having only one brain and only a certain number of working hours each day. If he had to depend on himself alone to make decisions and get things done, of course it would be impossible.

Stretch Your Brain

Today's wise businessman has learned to stretch his brain by using the minds of others to think out plans and problems in advance of having to make final decisions. I know of one top-level corporation officer who goes through a regular procedure in making decisions of major importance.

First, he calls in one or two aides and tells them of the problem, giving both the *pros* and the *cons* as he sees them. Then he ends with this sort of remark: "Now, I'm not going to tell you my opinion, partly because I'm not clear on the matter in my own mind, and partly because I want you to come up with your own independent ideas, after you've had a chance to dig up the facts."

When his subordinates come back with their views and reasons, it takes him just a few minutes to grasp their line of reasoning, and if it makes sense, he gives approval to their plan. Thus, he has saved himself hours and perhaps even days of study by substituting their brains for his own. If he finds an area which they have failed to explore in arriving at a conclusion, it is a simple matter to point out the importance of taking this into consideration and to ask them to go over the problem again.

Some Brains Are Better

There's another important advantage in using other people's brains: they may be better qualified than you to give an opinion in a particular situation. You'll agree, surely, that a man who works at a job day after day knows more about that job than anybody else. True, someone coming in fresh, with a new viewpoint, can often come up with a good suggestion. However, it is always smart to ask the man on the job for his opinion as to whether or not that suggestion will work. If the idea is good, nine times out of ten he will welcome it with enthusiasm. If it is not practical, he can tell you in two minutes why and where it will fall down.

I have seen this approach work miracles on problems which I thought defied solution.

Once we had a problem of incorrect counts in merchandise coming from Production into our Finished Goods Warehouse. No matter how much pressure we put on Production to make sure their counts were correct before releasing them to our warehouse manager, there was still considerable evidence that incorrect figures were slipping through. Even when we insisted that our warehouseman double-check each count, we still had errors.

Finally, our assistant warehouse foreman suggested that we have Production send down travel tickets directly to the Inventory Control Section without a copy to Warehousing. Then Warehousing was to make an independent count and send its ticket to Inventory Control, where both counts would be matched before being entered on our records. If there was a difference between the two counts, a re-count could be made before anything was shipped.

This new system worked like a charm. Our discrepancy problem was licked. And all because we listened to an assistant warehouse foreman who was close to the problem. He knew that whenever a warehouseman is busy, it is his natural inclination to accept unconsciously the count of the Production Department.

Watch For Prejudice

This sounds very good, you may be thinking. But what about those individuals who cannot or will not give you an opinion not biased by prejudices or personal ambitions? Yes, this is something you must always be conscious of in giving final approval to any plan suggested by subordinates.

To some extent, we are all biased. Sometimes, without knowing it ourselves, we give opinions colored by how we may fare personally in the outcome. But a keen executive instinctively brushes aside these personal prejudices to get at the real facts of the matter.

Often, just a brief word of caution will make an aide realize that he has not approached the problem from an over-all viewpoint. If this is done tactfully, he will quickly recognize the weakness of his position and alter his thinking accordingly.

Nearly all executives employ the technique of using the brains of others in administering their departments. What marks the difference between an average executive and one who is going to the top is usually the latter's ability to stimulate enthusiastic thinking among his subordinates.

How can this be done?

By giving them honest, sincere appreciation for their efforts, even if their ideas have to be modified or even discarded at a later date. Nothing will stifle a man's desire to think creatively faster than cruel, unthinking criticism of his ideas. You can always find something to praise in an idea, no matter how bad it appears at first.

Suggestion To Rockefeller

The story is told of an idea which one of John D. Rockefeller's partners had for making an investment in South America. It soon turned out that the investment was a bad one, and the firm lost a million dollars on the deal. John D. might have criticized him for the bad idea, but he did not want to kill the man's initiative for making suggestions in the future. So Rockefeller found something to praise. He congratulated the man because he had been able to save 60 percent of the money he had invested. "That's splendid," said Rockefeller; "we don't always do as well as that upstairs."

Praise is not only gratifying . . . it is the source of new energy that can be used for creative thinking by your subordinates. This will result in multiplying your accomplishments and those of your department.

Wiliam B. Given, Jr., President of American Brake Shoe Company, once said: "Sincere praise never hurts even the most conceited."

Charles Schwab said: "I don't need to criticize. When I don't praise, the men know something is wrong."

An actual measure of the energy that can be created through appreciation and praise was made by Dr. Henry H. Goddard at Vineland Training School in New Jersey. He used the *ergograph*, an instrument devised to measure fatigue. When an assistant said to a tired child at the instrument, "You're doing fine, John," the boy's energy-curve soared. Discouragement and fault-finding were found to have a measurable opposite effect.

Give Credit

Giving them credit, as we mentioned, is one very good way of using other people's minds to multiply your own brain power. Here's a true story to illustrate my point:

Cordell Hull came from the hills of Tennessee. His beginnings were almost as humble as Abraham Lincoln's. He became Secretary of State. He got a lot of things done by giving credit to others.

At one time, an influential Latin American official was very much anti-U.S. It was important to our Good Neighbor Policy that this man's country sponsor a certain phase of that policy. Here's how Cordell Hull worked it out:

"Mr. Minister," he said, at a big international conference, "we want the best man down here to put that program forward, so that we can give it our support. We hope you will do it; but, if you don't want to, we will get the next best man to do it."

The stubborn Latino was won over by the strategy of flattery and the knowledge that he would get credit. He proposed the matter, pushed it with his fellow diplomats . . . and Cordell Hull saw to it that this official got the credit.

Cordell Hull would have made a good business executive. He

knew how to influence people . . . as well as Dale Carnegie or almost anybody else on the recent scene.

William L. Batt, head of SKF Industries, is credited with the observation that "ability to influence people is the first requirement of an executive."

Alfred P. Sloan, when President of General Motors, said: "The most important thing I have learned about management is that an executive must arouse the individual initiative of the men working under him. Big business must be human if it is going to succeed, because what makes the wheels go round will always be human beings."

To Summarize

Encourage your subordinates to use their brains.

Don't be afraid to give credit for a good idea when it comes from a subordinate. A sure way to discourage positive thinking by your employees is to take credit personally for *their* ideas.

Remember, in the eyes of management, you will be given just as much credit for creating enough enthusiasm among your people, to get them to think up good ideas, as you would if you thought up each good idea yourself.

Another important point: In the final analysis, you will be judged on results. Your results will be far more noticeable if you learn and practice the technique of mutliplying your own brain power by using the brains of others.

You will need a lot of brains — including all of your own and whatever others you can command — if you are to become head of the firm before forty.

15

DON'T BE YOUR OWN WORST BOTTLENECK . . . ORGANIZE, DELEGATE, Then CHECK

American Airlines' President C. R. Smith, early in his company's history, often took a turn in the pilot's seat. Once when he was at the controls, something made a forced landing necessary. Smith put the plane down in a cornfield. Turning to his co-pilot, the chief of the young airline asked, "Well, what do you think?"

"I think you'd better let me do the flying and you run the air-line," was the blunt reply.

After that, Smith didn't do so much piloting, so the story goes . . . and American Airlines began expanding until it carried more passengers than any other airline in the world. Obviously, American Airlines could not have gone so far so fast if its president had continued spending a lot of his time flying airplanes.

When Donald Nelson was Chairman of the War Production Board during World War II, somebody remarked to him: "You must be the busiest man in the world."

"It's a pretty big job," replied Nelson (formerly head of Sears, Roebuck & Company), "but I don't have much to do. You see, my job is to make the other fellow work."

One can imagine that Donald Nelson had his tongue in his cheek, at least partway. The important point he was making, I believe, is: *Don't be afraid to delegate authority.*

Another way of looking at it: You've already made plenty of mistakes on your way up the business ladder. Now, give your sub-ordinates a chance. (Mahatma Gandhi, the great Indian leader, said: "Freedom is not worth having if it does not include the freedom to make mistakes.") Maybe your subordinates will do an even better job than you have been doing. Give them a chance.

Organization Is An Art

A later chapter deals with the "scientific attitude" in business. Some spheres of business, I believe, must be guided by attributes or innate gifts of personality surpassing in importance the mere knowledge and skills which come with the "scientific attitude." Organization is one of these spheres. It is an art, not a science.

Organization is the art which multiplies a one-man business enterprise into a large-scale, coordinated undertaking. Without organization — the controlled and directed teamwork of other people — there are distinct and rigid limits to what one man can do.

Skill in organizing can be developed to some degree. But there are some people who simply do not possess the talent to be a top-flight organizer. No matter how much training they receive, it seems they never quite get the hang of it.

Jack C. Vaughn, head of Spartan Drilling Company, an important force in Texas oil (and organizer of several other corporations), puts "organizational ability" at the top of his list of personal qualifications essential to gaining and holding a corporation presidency. I do not know of a corporation head who does not have organizational ability to a marked degree.

Take Time To Plan

Business growth requires people, always. The difference between a dry-goods store grossing $70,000 a year and a department store grossing $7,000,000 a year is largely a matter of organization. The merchant who personally unloads trucks, personally stocks his shelves, personally wraps packages, and acts as his own cashier — this man has that much less time for planning.

A pet shop operator sees an opportunity and sets up a wholesale department to sell to other pet shops and outlets that handle dog and cat food. Now he has people working for him: some selling, some delivering, and perhaps someone even buying for him. Without organization, he could not function effectively.

Jim and Fred both start out in the same line of business. Jim has exceptional talents in this field. During the early stages he quickly outstrips Fred, who is a plodder. But Jim does everything "important" himself, and eventually reaches a point where he can go no further because every waking hour of the day is used up. Fred, on the other hand, gradually acquires, trains, and organizes personnel. Eventually he passes Jim. He keeps on forging ahead. Oddly, the bigger his business grows, the more time he has for creative, forward planning. In short, Fred has an organization;

and, by delegating responsibility and authority, he has multiplied his effectiveness many-fold.

Hiring people is only one step in the organizing process. People must be welded into a unified whole, freed of overlapping and conflicting functions, held together by a common bond of morale. This takes organizing talent . . . but,

The Rewards Are Great

Organization relieves the businessman from slavish devotion to details. It enables him to work at his highest skill, managing his business.

Organization enables the top executive to coordinate the *four M's* — Men, Money, Machines, and Materials — retaining control over their use and performance, so that all factors in the business move ahead according to plan.

Organization is the key to eliminating waste materials and lost motion . . . and also the means of expanding opportunities for employees and executives.

Defined in another way, organization is *the wedding of authority and responsibility* . . . because, in its essentials, organization consists of assigning specific functions to designated people or departments, with authority for them to be carried out, plus accountability to management for the results obtained.*

We have seen the importance of organization and delegation to a young and growing business. Now, what happens when someone who does not have this ability walks into an operation which is already rather complex in its make-up? For awhile things will move along about the same as before. But soon the top man will ask for more and more matters to be brought to his attention before action is taken. Before long, his staff is afraid to move without the boss's approval. He becomes overworked. Important matters sit on his desk for days or weeks, awaiting his O.K. In short, he becomes his own worst bottleneck.

Administration By Delegation

John W. Thomas, for many years chief executive of Firestone Tire & Rubber Company, at first tried to handle all the details, but Harvey S. Firestone made him see how he would have to delegate authority. That's when Thomas started climbing the ladder at Firestone.

---

*Lasser, J. K.: *Business Management Handbook* (pp. 115-17).

It takes a certain amount of courage to delegate authority. One is always conscious of his own ultimate responsibility for the actions of his subordinates. But by training his people properly, and by setting up supervisory controls, the enlightened executive can accomplish much more through administration by delegation.

In many cases, subordinates can be relied upon for accuracy even more than the boss. I once had an honest boss who used to say, "I trust my people even more than I do myself, because they know more about what they are doing than I do."

Whenever one catches an employee in a mistake, the tendency is to think harshly about the individual's accuracy and ability. But just think how many mistakes you have made yourself . . . and perhaps with less difficult projects than those on which he is working.

The law of averages dictates that everyone will make some mistakes, and it is wise to have procedures that will catch as many as possible. But to be afraid to delegate authority simply because you are afraid mistakes will be made is folly indeed.

"Ideal" Planning

Several steps are involved in "ideal" organizational planning. These are:

1. *Determine Objectives.* "What are we aiming at?" is the beginning of wisdom in organizational planning. When specific goals or targets have been defined, only then is it possible to estimate what is required in the way of financing, facilities, personnel.

2. *Formulate Policies.* Administering a business depends for continuity and consistency upon the policies prescribed. At the top, policies are made or confirmed by the board of directors. At the departmental level, day-to-day policies are set up by the department head.

3. *Classify or Functionalize Operations.* Each function in an operation should be classified in order to determine where one ends and another begins. At top level, the four groups would be:

Finance
Production
Marketing
Accounting

In a department, each function will be less clear-cut but, if the department is large enough, a definite dividing line will be obvious.

4. *Departmentalize.* Once the separate functions become clear and their relations with others clearly understood, it is possible to set up departments or sections to handle particular functions. In addition to major functions, each may have one or more related minor functions. When organizing departments or sections within a department, due consideration should be given to administrative ease and control. Anything which needlessly increases the volume of reports, or which adds unnecessarily to the number of supervisors, impairs rather than improves business efficiency.

5. *Centralize Control.* The man at the top of any organizational structure should hold the reins or else have them held by someone under his direct supervision and control. The control function is largely a matter of records (plus interpretation) based on standards of performance.

6. *Recruit and Train Personnel.* The procurement, selection, and training of personnel, both supervisory and rank-and-file, are vital factors in building and maintaining an organization. Training should not only be directed at preparing the employee for the job at hand . . . ideally, every job should be regarded as an apprenticeship for something better. The department head who is not training his subordinates to undertake higher responsibilities is failing in his duty to them, himself, and to the firm.

The most important thing to remember about good organization is that its primary objectives are:

    (1) to permit delegation of authority, and
    (2) to exert control.

In other words, they provide answers to the questions: "Who is to do this work?" and "Is it being accomplished correctly at the right cost and on time?"*

If you want to maintain a steady climb up the executive ladder, it is absolutely essential that you develop the art of organization to the highest level possible. Without it, you will not only fail to make progress, but your day-to-day responsibilities will become bogged down around you until you become your own worst bottleneck.

Unless you learn, and learn early, to organize the efforts of those you supervise, so that you can more efficiently organize your own effort, and unless you learn to delegate authority — then don't count on being head of the firm before you're forty.

---

*Lasser, *op. cit.* (pp. 115-20).

16

BE THE KIND OF PERSON EVERYBODY LIKES

In most companies, large and small, the top man is usually liked and admired by more people than anyone at a lower executive level. This is not surprising when you consider that a person is selected for a company presidency partly because of his acceptability to the various individuals, groups, and departments which he must be able to lead and coordinate.

In the modern industrial complex, one of the most important organizational objectives of any company is to achieve a high degree of cooperation and teamwork. If a man has had difficulty getting along with people while assigned to smaller executive tasks, it is unlikely that he will ever get a chance at the top job, no matter what his other qualifications may be.

So, learn to get along smoothly with your fellow workers.

You don't have to be a hail-fellow-well-met. You do not have to be the-life-of-the-party. But it is important for you to be genuinely liked and respected.

An executive in his mid-thirties, who had a meteoric rise, once said to me: "I always try to avoid personality clashes. A man you criticize today may harbor a resentment for many years, and when he eventually gets a chance to slip in the knife, he will take great pleasure in twisting it vigorously."

Dale Carnegie, in the first chapter of his famous and justly popular book, *How To Win Friends And Influence People,* says: "Criticism is futile because it puts a man on the defensive. and usually makes him strive to justify himself. Criticism is dangerous, because it wounds a man's precious pride, hurts his sense of importance, and arouses his resentment."

Wise words from the most popular non-fiction book of our time. A bit further in the same chapter, Mr. Carnegie offers this excellent advice:

> It will probably take from now until Christmas to perfect yourself. You can then have a nice long rest over the holidays and devote the New Year to regulating and criticizing other people. But perfect yourself first.

Critic Not Always Right

It is significant to note how often the habitual critic is proved to be wrong after the other party has a chance to tell his side of the story. But the damage is done, once the criticism is made. The critic has created an enemy who will wait patiently for an opportunity to get even.

Some time ago my firm hired a new accounting executive. He was a very brilliant man and I wondered why he had not gone further in his previous companies. He worked hard and did a remarkable job of revitalizing our accounting set-up. But he had an unfortunate habit which seemed to hold him back like a heavy leash.

Whenever he became a bit fatigued, he would start to complain out loud about his subordinates, or about inefficiency in other departments supplying him with data. I have, on several such occasions, walked over to his desk and said, "Well, let's look into this thing and try to get it straightened out once and for all." Then, after we started to check out all the documents involved, we found that everything had been done exactly in line with company policy. He simply had not taken the time to check thoroughly before jumping to the conclusion that someone else had erred.

You know such people. Plutarch, the ancient Greek, knew some of them, and had them in mind when he wrote: "To find fault is easy; to do better may be difficult."

Even if someone else does make a mistake, it is usually better to go directly to that person and work it out rather than publicize the error throughout the company. In this way, you will not only correct the mistake for the good of your company, but — in most cases — you will earn the other person's undying gratitude.

Pull Yourself UP — Don't Push Others DOWN

It's a common human fault to try to elevate yourself by pushing another down. It works that way with groups, with nations, with races, and with individuals.

If you are like most other people, you are often tempted to show yourself superior by finding and announcing someone else's error. I had just such an experience early in my career, when I was doing market research.

The project required my collaboration with the head of our Advertising Research Section. We worked for many weeks setting up a program to test the advisability of introducing a cream shampoo under the same name as our leading liquid shampoo. Finally, the test was put into the works and data was obtained for presentation to top executives. Part of the report was to be written by me, and the other part by the other section head.

Two days after the report was released, I happened to be going over some of the same data for a second analysis. I sensed something was wrong with the advertising figures, so I checked them out and found a big error which would change the conclusion significantly.

My first impulse was to run in and tell our department head. After all (the little green devil in my head was telling me), I had been on the job only a little more than a year, and it would be a feather in my cap to catch someone else of more experience in an error of this magnitude.

For some reason, however, I decided instead to go directly to the other section head — the man responsible for that part of the report. He was mortified. The report had been discussed already, in Executive Committee. It would be embarrassing to him. It would be embarrassing to the entire Marketing Research Department. He was in a spot.

But, he was man enough to do the right thing for the company. He asked me if he might tell our boss, the head of the department. I gave that little green devil (in my head) a push to the rear, and agreed that my friend should reveal his own error. He reported it to our department head. The subject never came up again, to my knowledge.

I have not seen this man since I left that company. He is now a high executive in the TV and Radio Section of their Advertising Department. But, I can't help thinking that he bears me no grudge today, as he most surely would if I had obeyed my first impulse to run to the boss with the evidence of what could have been interpreted as incompetence. And, actually, he was far from incompetent, as later developments have proved. He simply made a mistake, just the same as I have made hundreds of mistakes in the years I have been working for a living . . . and you will make them too.

How Lincoln Did It

When you do have occasion, or necessity, to bring a mistake to the attention of a subordinate or a co-worker, do it in such a way as to avoid resentment. The best way I know to avoid resentment is to start off by praising the one you must correct.

Abraham Lincoln used this technique on many occasions, but perhaps never so effectively as he did on April 26, 1863, during the darkest period of the Civil War. For nearly a year and a half the Union Army had gone from one defeat to another. The nation was so appalled that many influential members of Congress were calling for Lincoln's resignation.

Some of the trouble was due to the actions of obstreperous Major General Joseph Hooker. Lincoln felt compelled to try to change some of Hooker's grave faults. But he did not call them grave faults. Even in this letter, written at a time when the very fate of the nation might depend on the General's actions, Lincoln found it possible to praise Hooker:

> I have placed you at the head of the Army of the Potomac. Of course, I have done this upon what appears to me to be sufficient reasons, and yet I think it best for you to know that there are some things in regard to which I am not quite satisfied with you.
>
> I believe you to be a brave and skillful soldier, which, of course, I like. I also believe you do not mix politics with your profession, in which you are right. You have confidence in yourself, which is valuable if not an indispensable quality.
>
> You are ambitious, which, within reasonable bounds, does good rather than harm. But I think that during General's Burnside's command of the Army you have taken counsel of your ambition and thwarted him as much as you could, in which you did a great wrong to the country and to a most meritorious and honorable brother officer.
>
> I have heard, in such a way as to believe it, of your recently saying that both the Army and the Government needed a dictator. Of course, it was not for this, but in spite of it, that I have given you command.
>
> Only those generals who gain successes can set up as dictators. What I now ask of you is military success and I will risk the dictatorship.
>
> The Government will support you to the utmost of its ability, which is neither more nor less than it has done and will do for all commanders. I much fear that the spirit which you have aided

to infuse into the army, of criticizing their commander and with-holding confidence from him, will now turn upon you. I shall assist you, as far as I can, to put it down.

Neither you nor Napoleon, if he were alive again, could get any good out of an army while such spirit prevails in it; and now beware of rashness. Beware of rashness, but with energy and sleepless vigilance go forward and give us victories.

Be Natural — Be Yourself

While it is important to be liked and admired, you should never try to accomplish this by socializing beyond what is normal for your position in the company. Occasionally, I hear of an ambitious young man who is trying to gain recognition by enter-taining all the "right" people. It never really helps very much, because this kind of socializing is not natural, and the purpose soon becomes obvious to both the entertained and those who observe the practice from the sidelines. From either direction, it does not tend to make the entertainer any more popular.

Also, a disproportionate amount of socializing can hurt you in an even more direct way. Many bosses tend to judge their sub-ordinates partly by observing the way they manage their personal financial matters. If you spend more than a normal amount on entertaining, it is just a matter of time before the strain will be felt in your pocketbook (more on this in a later chapter). Carried to the extreme, this can result in serious deficits in your budget, causing you to borrow against future earnings, and in other ways to get yourself out on a financial limb. At best, it does not enhance your boss's opinion of you if he gets the idea you spend lavishly on entertainment.

Work At It

Being the kind of person other people like is something you will have to work at, if you're like the rest of us. Since our chief interest is ourselves, it doesn't come natural to us to *show* a great deal of interest in the other fellow, without trying. But, to be-come the kind of person other people like a great deal, we must show interest in them . . . and without appearing to try. It must be a natural, spontaneous, sincere kind of interest, too.

Thus, *being liked* comes as a product of actively and whole-heartedly *liking others*. You have to start with that. Just learning some pat formula for popularity won't do the trick for you. You won't have to look very far in 'how-to-be-happy" books to find such pat formulas . . . all of them good, when put to work.

In *How To Win Friends And Influence People,* Dale Carnegie sets down these "Six Ways to Make People Like You":

1. Become genuinely interested in other people.
2. Smile.
3. Remember that a man's name is to him the sweetest and most important sound in the English language.
4. Be a good listener. Encourage others to talk about themselves.
5. Talk in terms of the other man's interest.
6. Make the other person feel important — and do it sincerely.

This is the best formula I've ever found for making people like you. I recommend it to you without reservation, just as I highly recommend Dale Carnegie's entire book to you, not only for reading but for *re*-reading, study, and application. It will help you, I know; it has helped millions.

Summarizing —

To get to the top of a modern corporation, it is vital to:

. . . make yourself acceptable to and liked by everybody you deal with, insofar as this is humanly possible;

. . . learn to *get along* with others, though their views and ideas may be quite different from your own;

. . . find your own faults (and correct them) — if you must find fault with somebody;

. . . pull others UP with you; you can't rise very far by pushing others down;

. . . avoid resentment toward yourself by tempering criticism with praise;

. . . watch your budget (money, time, and health) when it comes to socializing.

Those are some of the points worth watching as you properly exercise your social nature and sociable inclinations on your way to the top . . . and remember, you *must* watch things like that if you are to become head of the firm before you're forty.

17

STAY OUT OF COMPANY POLITICS
And You'll Be Facing Fewer Critics

One of the thorniest problems of getting along in a corporation is office politics. There is active politicking at every level of business, from the typing pool to the executive suite . . . no use denying it. People of similar interests and desires will always get together informally to protect their interests or promote their aspirations. You'll waste your time if you spend it trying to change this basic human trait.

The two main goals of company politics are:

(1) to obtain information;
(2) to influence the boss.

Let's see how it works.

Typical Example

Mr. A, in Accounting, becomes friendly with Mr. B, in Purchasing. Both happen to think that Mr. C, in Marketing, is squandering the firm's money with his reckless ideas for introducing new products. They would rather see some economies introduced into the sales force and a more conservative policy on expansion. Mr. C, however, has an ally, Mr. D, in the Research Department, and perhaps another in the Production Department. They have visions of a greatly expanded company, with more volume and more profits. They cannot understand why some people in the company are dragging their feet when *they* work night and day for a bigger and better organization.

So far, this difference of opinion is not damaging. Actually, it is helpful to have different viewpoints on a policy of this magnitude.

It helps point out weaknesses, and gives the company an opportunity to strengthen the program before too much money is spent.

If the idea turns out a flop, it helps to have people who are strong enough to call attention to the failure, and to suggest a halt before additional funds are expanded on a project that has little chance for success. As a matter of fact, in most instances an idea is not all good or all bad. Usually, there are a few elements of both good and bad inherent in the initial plan. A little pushing and pulling from opposite directions is invaluable to those responsible for making the ultimate decision, because it adds some much-needed balance to the thinking and planning.

Unfortunately, however, office politics does not often let the difference of opinion stop right there. Too often, it goes into a second stage, which can be illustrated by a continuation of our example.

Mr. A asks Mr. B to keep him advised of any requests made by Mr. C for new product components or promotional material. When a request for something directly traceable to the new project comes to Mr. B's desk, he makes it a point to talk with Mr. A, both of them deploring the kind of thinking that would permit such goings-on in their company. Whenever either gets opportunity to put in a dig, they do so with great glee. They ignore the fact that their criticism in the presence of subordinates can only result in disunity. In their determined effort to discredit the idea and the people who are responsible for it, they may even occasionally make a negative remark in front of the boss.

Mr. C has become aware of this campaign, however. He gets together with Mr. D, to compare notes and plan a counter-campaign. Thus, in an informal way, both sides have set up listening posts to get information in activities of the other. This information is used in various ways to support their own position, and to tear down the ideas of the opposing camp.

Politics Is Shaky Foundation

Needless to say, office politics of this kind can be extremely harmful to a company. Not only does it destroy teamwork but, carried to the extreme, it can result in one side trying to prove the other side wrong, even if they do not honestly believe it. Too bad that so many corporations are plagued by this unhealthy variety of politics.

A person who allows himself to be caught up in vicious office politics is building for his career a foundation that is very shaky indeed. Office politics may help him progress temporarily, but sooner or later his allies will either lose prestige or they may find it advantageous to court the favor of some other bright young person who can do them more good. This could happen to you. If it does, and if your progress has been based on such an alliance, your castle of success might come tumbling down. Don't let that happen to you.

It Has Happened

I know of several instances where exactly this did happen. One case had its beginning when I was on my first job. Its final chapter was written just a few years ago.

There was a brilliant young man in our department, and many of us knew he would go a long way. He had intelligence, charm, good looks, and outstanding business instinct. But, he also had a habit of creating artificially close associations with those in positions to do him some good. Moreover, while cultivating these people, he ignored or even antagonized practically all others, particularly those not especially esteemed by people of greatest prestige in the department. I remember how he praised our department head to a degree that was almost sycophantic, even worshipful by appearance. Similarly, he had sugared words for one of our section heads who, rumor had it, was slated for a bigger job.

After I left the company, I was not surprised to hear that this young man made rapid strides up the executive ladder. From all indications, it appears that he had helped push upstairs several key men who, in turn, pulled him up.

But I started to recognize the pattern when, four or five years ago, I met him at a trade convention. I asked about various men we both had known in the company. I was amazed. What had once been outspoken praise for the man under whom we had served had now turned to virtual vilification. He criticized our former boss severely. I could only interpret this as my friend's recognition that the man we both once admired was on his way out. Two months later, my suspicions were confirmed. Our erstwhile department head resigned, and my young friend moved up to a position of even greater prestige and responsibility.

Then, two years ago, I received another bit of news about my old company. It seemed to substantiate my theory on the flimsiness of a career built on office politics. My young friend had been caught in a shake-up of top and middle management. Most of his former allies were removed from posts of great responsibility and he, of course, was reduced in position along with the rest of them. I first heard that this job had been abolished. Then, six months later, it was reinstated — with another man in his old position. While he is still with the company, or was the last time I heard, my young friend's prestige has been greatly reduced.

First Loyalty To Company

Benjamin Fairless, who became head of U. S. Steel at 48, is one of the most distinguished self-made corporation presidents in American business history. In an article in *Life* Magazine (October 15, 1956) he tells of his first brush with company politics, which convinced him of the importance of keeping clear of this pitfall.

The two top men of United States Steel had a clash that eventually resulted in one of them leaving the company. At that time Mr. Fairless was subordinate to both of them. But he refused to take sides, even after Mr. X had left the firm. A few years later, the differences were patched up, and Mr. X returned to U. S. Steel. Benjamin Fairless, of course, was then in a stronger position than ever, because he had not deserted either man during the period of strained relations. His loyalty remained exactly where it should have been . . . with the company.

Politicians LOSE Favor

A seasoned executive will usually recognize the symptoms of unreasonable politicking. And, usually, he will take it into consideration when making decisions about promotions. Furthermore, a person with a reputation for being a company politician will eventually lose favor with his superiors. They recognize the importance of discipline and loyalty within an organization; they don't want to have an ambitious young upstart destroying the teamwork they have worked so hard to build.

One time I received a long-distance phone call from St. Louis, where a crew of our salesmen were doing some missionary selling. I was vice president for sales at the time, and the person calling was a young salesman who wanted permission to come to Home Office for a talk about the crew manager. It seemed that my caller and some of the other men didn't like the way the crew manager was handling the campaign. I told this salesman not to come on company time, or at company expense. I told him, furthermore, that he was responsible directly to the crew manager, who would be judged by results. I used as much tact as I could. I did not want to kill the man's enthusiastic spirit. But perhaps I overplayed this part; for over the next weekend this very same man, accompanied by a co-worker of like mind, flew to Home Office at his own expense.

My first impulse was to refuse to talk to them. Later events proved that this might have been the better course. However, I consented to a Saturday afternoon appointment. I heard them tell bitter stories about how all the work was being done by the salesmen, with little help from the crew manager. They went on to point out their boss's ineptness, and how money was being wasted in St. Louis.

I knew certain parts of their story were factual. But I had no choice but to put them back on a plane for St. Louis to be ready for work at 8:30 Monday morning. I could not afford to destroy the discipline of our entire organization by allowing subordinates to cut across lines of authority whenever they had a gripe, legitimate or not.

Furthermore, I had less enthusiasm for the two who did not have enough respect for our organizational structure to go through channels when attempting to rectify what they felt to be wrong. Not surprisingly, perhaps, one of them resigned six months later; and the other, the more aggressive of the two, later tangled with another superior over travel expenses and was finally let out of the company. Even then, he could not leave clean, but determined to cause still more upheaval by writing a letter directly to our chairman of the board, criticizing everyone from the top right on down.

Company politics can be a damaging thing to any firm. It can be even more damaging to the person who tries to build his career foundation on the shifting sands of loyalty to a clique rather than to the company itself.

If you expect to become head of your firm, before or after forty, you'd better build your future on something more solid than office politics.

18

CULTIVATE THE "SCIENTIFIC ATTITUDE"

Andrew Carnegie, one of America's most successful businessmen, etablished some high marks at which others will be shooting for a long, long time. In his later years, when he was giving away millions for education, public libraries, and other public-spirited projects, he got the idea that success in business could be reduced to a science. He chose Napoleon Hill to organize and set down this "science of success."

Mr. Hill devoted considerable time and creative thought to this most interesting project. He drew heavily from Mr. Carnegie's own philsophy, and from the great steel-maker's record of accomplishment. He also drew from the records and thoughts of more than 500 other top-ranking business and professional men.

One product of this fruitful study was a book titled *How To Raise Your Own Salary,* to which we referred in Chapter 5. In that book are set forth Andrew Carnegie's Seventeen Principles:

1. Definiteness of Purpose.
2. The Master Mind (cultivate the spirit of harmony).
3. Attractive Personality.
4. Applied Faith.
5. The Extra Mile.
6. Organized Individual Endeavor.
7. Creative Vision.
8. Self-Discipline.
9. Organized Thought.
10. Learn from Defeat.
11. Seek Inspiration (Enthusiasm Applied).
12. Control Attention.

13. Apply the Golden Rule.
14. Cooperation.
15. Budget Time and Money.
16. Good Health.
17. Cosmic Habit-force.

In half a century there has been a slight shift in emphasis, apparently, in what successful business men believe to be the main ingredients of their own success. Compare Carnegie's Seventeen Principles with the list of major factors given in Chapter 1. Several points are identical, of course, though different words are used. Note that "planned public relations," relatively important to today's successful executive, received no mention in Mr. Hill's study. Neither did "opportunism," "luck," or some of the other factors regarded as important by some of today's most outstanding up-and-coming corporation heads.

"Scientific Attitude" Gains Popularity

Yet the basic concept of the scientific attitude toward business has remained strong . . . in fact, it has gained in strength in the half-century since Andrew Carnegie and Napoleon Hill helped to popularize the idea.

The scientific attitude in business got a big push in 1903, when Frederick W. Taylor (see also Chapter 10) proposed and instituted a system of shop management under the term *scientific management*. (You'll find it described briefly in Webster's Unabridged Dictionary, and in great detail in Mr. Taylor's writings.)

My own feeling is that perhaps the best summation of "the scientific attitude" is that suggested by John Ruskin, the 19th-century English writer and professor of art at Oxford University: "Having or seeking precise knowledge or information." Just *getting the facts . . .* that's it.

Kenneth Keyes, Jr., previously quoted, has some timely thoughts on the "scientific attitude" in business, in his book *How To Develop Your Thinking Ability*:

> It is impossible to achieve a high average in batting out sound business decisions without the scientific attitude. The scientific attitude is a useful in running a business as in running a scientific laboratory. In both, it is fact, not fancy, that enables us to think straight and find what really works. The scientific method helps us meet new situations without making fools of ourselves. And *up to a point* every situation in life is a new situation — different in time, different in place, and different in the individuals and

things involved. We cannot use the scientific method in making ALL our decisions, but when making our most important ones, we should remember that it is the most useful method known to help us turn up facts we need to make sound decisions *that will apply to present conditions.**

Let The Facts Speak . . . Correctly

But, contrary to the popular saying, facts do not always speak for themselves. They must be analyzed logically in relation to the problem at hand. Often what they seem to say is a costly deception.

To demonstrate how this can happen, let's take the example of a leading department store. Top management had been considering a huge investment in modernizing its old-fashioned interiors. Studies were made of other department stores where remodeling had paid off in large sales increases. It seemed natural to assume that the same would happen if they modernized with new fixtures and new lighting.

The head of the Woman's Wear Department was particularly aggressive and pushed for quick approval of a plan to modernize throughout . . . including a new emphasis on high fashion and aggressive promotion gimmicks. For a few weeks after remodeling, sales increased. Then they began a gradual but continuing decline. An outside consultant found the facts that management had overlooked.

Many customers were women who had long bought nearly all their clothes in the Women's Apparel Department. What these women had liked most about the store was its old-fashioned atmosphere. A simple but well-designed survey revealed that they felt uncomfortable in the jazzy atmosphere of the newly-remodeled department. Consequently, they did not come to the store so often as before. This caused a drop in sales, not only in that department, but in others as well.

When the former decor was restored, the firm's business gradually picked up. Meanwhile, sizeable sums had been lost in sales and wasted decoration costs. Had the facts been assembled and had they been analyzed in relation to conditions in that store and at that time, these losses would have been avoided.

On The Right Track

Here's an example of how a scientific attitude can help a

---

*Kenneth Keyes, Jr.: *How To Develop Your Thinking Ability* (McGraw-Hill, 1950).

smart business executive keep on the right track:

A large food company was planning to re-design the package of its fastest-moving product. One smart young man in Marketing Research pleaded for a detailed consumer study before management made up its mind definitely to tamper with the package. He first asked the executives responsible for the decision to establish the requirements of the new package. After some prompting, they finally said the new package must:

(1) compete effectively for consumer attention at the point of sale;
(2) exemplify high quality and encourage purchase;
(3) gain widespread recognition as typifying the brand.

Once these requirements were established, the next step was to determine how well the present package fulfilled them. A comprehensive study was undertaken on each point. The old package scored high in each.

What resulted? Instead of a completely new design, the firm made only two small changes which, the studies had shown, would make the package score even higher. Thus a rational, balanced design was substituted for a major overhaul that might well have resulted in a catastrophic loss of identity for the product. Needless to say, the young marketing analyst is now being listened to with more respect.

Base Judgment On Fact

All of us have the idea that our judgment is pretty good . . . at least most of the time. And perhaps it is. But to a young man who wants to establish a reputation for making sound decisions, there is no substitute for the scientific attitude. True, you will not always have the time to make a painstaking study of each problem before rendering a decision. But, always you will find facts available, limited as they may be, to help you keep your thinking on the right track.

Sometimes these facts can be found in records. Sometimes they should be picked from the minds of your subordinates. In other instances, you'll simply have to go out and dig them up. However, if you balance the importance of the decision against the time you spend assembling facts, you'll find that a little extra effort to be sure of your ground will pay off in big dividends right now and in the years to come.

My first job after college was to conduct sales tests for merchandising managers (now known as "brand men") of one of the nation's larger soap companies. My best customer was a young man who had worked for the company in Poland and was brought over to this country after the Nazis took over in 1939. His English was still somewhat broken, but his mind was as sharp as any in the entire home office. What's more, he handled one of the company's most important products — a tremendous responsibility under any circumstances. But somehow he managed to push the item higher and higher in the "share of market" sweepstakes. And, surprisingly, he seemed to do it without spending disproportionate sums for advertising.

His Secret: Testing

It was obvious to me how he was able to perform near-miracles in a market that was noted for dog-eat-dog policies on the part of all three leading competitors. He made it a cardinal rule to test every idea . . . from new design for a display carton to a major revision in pricing policy.

I recall one time he asked me to run a store audit test on banding three cakes of soap together in a multiple pack. Up until this time it had been the custom to run half-price sales with multiple packs, and invariably these special deals resulted in extra consumer sales . . . at least during the period of the promotion. But, this marketing executive wanted to know something more than what was already known to everyone in the soap business. He wanted to know *why*. Was it because the lower price attracted the shopper? Or was some other factor playing a motivating role?

He asked me to set up a sample of stores in which the product would be banded but no change in retail price would be put into effect. In other words, Mrs. Consumer would be confronted with three bars of soap strapped together in a single package, but the price of the package would be exactly the same as if she purchased the three bars separately.

To my great astonishment, an increase in sales was achieved that was not significantly different from the increase where a special price was in effect. My astute friend had suspected that a psychological factor was at work encouraging consumers to buy three bars where they might normally buy only one. And with no savings either.

Now, here's the moral:

Even though he had a good idea of the eventual answer, he first subjected it to testing before using it in his merchandising plan.

This is just another way of saying that he believed in applying a scientific attitude to his business problems. (P.S. If you happen to meet this man today and ask for his card, you'll see that his title is vice president.)

Stuck . . . With Facts

Sometimes even experienced executives get the cart before the horse when making business decisions. The president of a firm which manufactures a line of adhesives hit on an idea to dispense a glue in a new and different kind of container. He called in designers and described what he wanted. After the new design had been produced, along with a couple of alternatives suggested by the designers, he agreed to test it in the market before going into production. This was most fortunate, because the new design proved to have poor appeal.

At this point, the firm finally got around to doing what they should have done as a first step. They started analyzing the problem and determining the information needed. Two questions soon became obvious: Who were the potential buyers? and, What sort of container would appeal most to them?

The answer to the first was readily available to them. Most users of this type of glue were women — housewives and office workers. The answer to the second was provided by a sample survey, testing different types of containers. The one originally suggested by the company president appealed strongly to men, but not at all to women. When a design was found that had an equivalent appeal to women, the item was put on the market and achieved a rapid commercial success. The new design stuck . . . it was based on facts.

To Summarize

I must agree wholeheartedly with Kenneth Keyes, Jr., when he says a scientific attitude is vital if you want to achieve a favorable average in making sound business decisions. As a possible future candidate for a corporation presidency, you will do well to start early and get in the habit of making decisions based on facts. Even when you have all the facts, you must analyze them carefully in the light of present conditions and objectives. Then you'll have a better-than-even chance to come up with the right answer. And remember, a high percentage of right answers is essential to a man on his way to becoming head of the firm before forty.

19

BE AN ACTIVE CITIZEN
Know How To Defend Free Enterprise

It stands to reason that any man contemplating becoming the head of a business enterprise should be able to defend the free enterprise system against all comers. Let's face it — we live at a time when the free enterprise system has come under heavy attack from many quarters: intellectuals, socialists, government bureaucrats, and, of course, the Communists. Regardless of how brilliantly successful free enterprise has been in satisfying the needs of man and bringing civilization to unprecedented heights of advancement, there are people who would do away with this system and turn the clock back. These people may not be many, but somehow they manage to gain enough political power to make it possible for them to take over an entire country — as they did in Cuba — and destroy the free enterprise system.

In The Front Lines

The businessman, therefore, is in the front lines of this battle between two ways of life, and he automatically becomes a spokesman for the system which has made his success possible. But being a good businessman and knowing how to defend the free enterprise system in sound philosophical and moral terms are two separate abilities. Believe it or not, many a good businessman who could outwit his competitors in a dozen clever ways, has been caught at a loss when confronted with the arguments of a collectivist or an advocator of greater government controls. The advantages of the free enterprise system have seemed so obvious to him, that he assumed everybody else felt the same way. Thus he never bothered to study or be well versed in the philosophical and moral premises of the very system in which he has built his carreer. How can the businessman be prepared for such intellectual confrontations? By boning up on the subject of free-market economics and the history of capitalism.

Organizations Help

Fortunately there are a number of organizations dedicated to disseminating knowledge about the free enterprise system to which the young executive can go for help. The Foundation for Economic Education is one of them. Located at Irvington-on-Hudson, New York, the Foundation was created for the specific purpose of educating people about the free enterprise system. Many business executives and company presidents subscribe to its publications and a number of top corporation executives are on its Board of Trustees.

Other businessmen, already well-versed in the principles of capitalism, have taken it upon themselves to educate the public about the free enterprise system. For example, Joe Crail, President of Coast Federal Savings in Los Angeles, the third largest savings and loan association in the United States, has incorporated in his company's public relations program the publication of numerous colorful booklets and pamphlets about the free enterprise system.

Individual Action

Another such active businessman is Fred C. Koch, president of Rock Island Oil & Refining Company, Inc., and director of six other corporations. Koch helped organize the Winkler-Koch Engineering Company of Wichita, Kansas, in 1925. This company specialized in the design and erection of petroleum refineries. In 1929, 1930, and 1931 Winkler-Koch built fifteen oil-cracking plants in the Soviet Union. It was during his visit to the U.S.S.R. that Koch became aware of the seriousness of the Communist plan to destroy the free enterprise system in the United States. Ever since then, Koch has been actively engaged in defending the free enterprise system by writing articles, speaking before business and civic groups, and participating in educational programs with other businessmen.

Another organization started by businessmen to help defend the free enterprise system is the American Security Council of Chicago, Illinois. This organization was founded by business so that it might be better informed and thus more effective in meeting its cold war responsibilities. Among the members of the Council's Senior Advisory Board are such corporation heads as Bennett Archambault, Chairman of the Stewart-Warner Corporation; Robert W. Galvin, President of Motorola, Incorporated, and Wayne A. Johnston,

President of the Illinois Central Railroad.

It is obvious, therefore, from the foregoing, that businessmen have a vital role to play in the field of educating the public on the crucial issue of free enterprise versus communism and socialism. Many former Cuban businessmen now in the United States have taken to the lecture platform to teach Americans about the American way of life and how to protect it.

In Politics, Too

In the field of domestic politics, businessmen have learned that they too have an important role to play. Businessmen as individuals have long been contributors to the campaign funds of their preferred candidates in both political parties. In 1963, however, a group of business executives decided to become more active in politics and formed the Business-Industry Political Action Committee (BIPAC). The organization was formed to provide financial support to Congressional candidates of both parties who support the free enterprise system and the philosophy of individualism. Some of the business executives on its Board of Directors are Clifford J. Backstrand, Chairman of the Board of the Armstrong Cork Company; Samuel M. Fleming, President of the Third National Bank of Nashville; and H. C. Lumb, Vice President of the Republic Steel Corporation.

Many of the businessmen who participate in these activities derive a great deal of benefit for themselves and their companies. Not only do they learn more about how the American system works, but they make contacts with other businessmen from many different parts of the country and enlarge their scope of acquaintances. In some lines of business, participation in public affairs can and no doubt will directly benefit your firm. Whatever the nature of your business, you're sure to derive considerable personal benefit.

Be A Joiner

Benjamin Franklin, who was signally successful in business as well as in diplomacy and other phases of government, suggested one of his secrets in his *Autobiography*:

> I had now just passed my twenty-first year. I now set up in partnership with Meredith, one of Keimer's workmen. the money being found by Meredith's father. In the autumn of the preceding year, I had formed most of my ingenious acquaintance into a club of mutual improvement, which we called the Junto . . . Every one of its members exerted himself in recommending business to our new firm.

I now set on foot my first project of a public nature, that for a subscription library. By the help of our club, the Junto, I procured fifty subscribers of forty shillings each to begin with, and ten shillings a year for fifty years. We afterwards obtained a charter, and this was the mother of all the North American subscription libraries now so numerous, which have made the common tradesmen and farmers as intelligent as most gentlemen. . . .

Our secret club, the Junto, had turned out to be so useful that I now set every member of it to form each of them a subordinate club, with the same rules, but without informing the new clubs of their connexion with the Junto. The advantages proposed were, the improvement of so many young citizens; our better acquaintance with the general sentiments of the inhabitants on any occasion, as the Junto member was to report to the Junto what passed in his separate club; the promotion of our particular interests in business by more extensive recommendation; and the increase of our influence in public affairs.

Benjamin Franklin's "influence in public affairs," at home and abroad, was not by accident. It began with the fact that he was an *active* citizen, from early years.

Leroy Wilson, who was to rise to presidency of American Telephone & Telegraph Company, was in engineering school when he became aware that he had not had very much experience in getting along with people (he was an only child) and needed to know something about leadership, firsthand. He became a Boy Scout troop leader. Years later he said that this marked the start of his climb, which took him to the top of the world's largest private enterprise.

A Delicate Subject

A subject seldom explored in depth — and which I shall barely touch on — is the very delicate subject of *morality and taxes*. You'll find plenty volumes in your library, and plenty of felons in prisons, because of different approaches to the *legality* of taxes, but I have yet to find any recorded discussion of the moral aspects of tax practices.

As you progress higher and higher in your firm, you will be confronted, some fine morning in March, with tax questions which are not entirely legal in nature. The legal answer may be fairly clear. The moral answer may not be quite so clear. The legal answer will satisfy Uncle Sam. Maybe that will be sufficient answer for you, as well.

The only point I make here is: *Being a good citizen, you will be confronted with moral questions as well as legal ones.* You'll want to have answers for both kinds.

Join Trade and Professional Associations . . .
Membership Can Add To Your Qualifications

Being an active citizen includes being active within your own industry or profession. Trade and professional associations in your particular line of business can immeasurably help you, if you'll join and help them. A questionnaire addressed to several score executive officers of trade and professional associations across the United States included this question:

> *About what percentage of your most active members have received promotions within their own companies since becoming active in your association?*

Answers ranged from 20% to 85%, with a simple average of 37%. Most of the executives answering this question stated that their most active members are now either presidents or vice presidents of their own firms.

C. Harry Christopher, Executive Secretary of Hotel Greeters of America, stated: "We have direct evidence that young men and women, through Greeter activity, have been given advancement in their profession, because their interest has been noted by the top men in the industry and promotions have followed. One general manager of a large hotel in the South, who has been in the same hotel for fifty-five years, rising from bellboy to his present position, publicly gives the Greeter organization credit for his advancement, and we can cite many other examples."

Representative of benefits offered the individual by such trade and professional associations are these listed by the *American Gas Association*: "To provide methods of education for its members, their employees and others interested in the gas industry; to encourage educational programs by others, and to maintain a clearing house of information and facilities for study in various fields of the gas industry . . . (and to provide) Opportunity for your company employees to attend and address national meetings and thereby increase their stature."

Some trade and professional associations offer placement services for individual members . . . something which can be quite beneficial if and when you decide to make another connection.

The chief executive of an association with some seven hundred company members said that about 85 percent of the individuals most active in his association have received promotions since becoming active in the association, and that most of these industry leaders are now vice presidents in their own firms. He stated that about 25 percent of individual members are active in voluntarily suggesting or soliciting new members . . . a relatively high degree of enthusiasm — which has a bearing, no doubt, on the 85-percent personal promotion figure.

I addressed another questionnaire to outstanding young corporation presidents, and on a question concerning membership in trade and professional associations, four out of five rated such activity "important" in their own climb up the executive ladder. Strong testimony to the value of membership in trade and professional associations.

Help "Clean Up"

There's always some "cleaning up" to be done . . . within your industry, in your own neighborhood, or in the larger sphere of state or national government. So, make politics one of your avocations. You may find it more satisfying than golf, less expensive than yachting . . . and it could be tied in with both, to your profit. Plato said, "The punishment suffered by the wise who refuse to take part in the government, is to live under the government of bad men." Never content yourself with living under that sort of government.

Help your industry, help your community, help yourself . . . be an *active* citizen. As James La Bagnara (dynamic young head of Precision Gears & Products Company, Paterson, New Jersey) points out: "It's very important . . . keeps your name and personality in the papers." Which suggests some of the sweeter uses of publicity, touched on in another chapter.

As Plato suggested . . . unless you're to live under the government of bad men, you'll have to do something about it yourself. You'll have to be at least a bit active in politics. Politics . . . on the local, state, or national level . . . always will be as clean or as dirty as the people practicing this art of government (it is not a science, as Daniel Webster so effectively pointed out). If some "cleaning up" is in order in your bailiwick, maybe you'd make a good cleanup man.

So, take time . . . or make time . . . to be an active citizen. You won't have to look for opportunities in public affairs; just open your eyes . . . the opportunities are right there, waiting for you. Don't put it off until after you're forty. Start being an active citizen now, on your way up . . . it should help you go up faster, on your way to becoming head of your firm before forty.

20

DON'T LET YOURSELF DOWN BY LIVING IT UP

"Sure I entertain lavishly and live expensively. But it's a good investment in my future."

The young junior executive was explaining why it was difficult for him to make ends meet. He was voicing an opinion held by many ambitious young men who believe they can spend their way to success via the social route.

Nothing could be farther from the truth! As a matter of fact, living at a social level beyond your reasonable financial means can have the exactly opposite effect — it can ruin your chances for a high-level job.

A reasonable amount of socializing is beneficial, of course, and necessary in the development of any kind of career. Contacts are important. What better atmosphere in which to make them than under circumstances of sociability? Furthermore, you will get to know your superiors and your co-workers better under conditions where both you and they are relaxed. This can lead to smoother relationships in your working week, and thereby help you climb the executive ladder faster. But when socializing takes on the form of lavish entertaining or living beyond your means, the inevitable result *must* be disaster. Let me illustrate.

High Living Kept Him Down

A young executive in the sales department of a toiletry manufacturing firm was bent on getting ahead. He started to "cultivate" the men he felt could be most helpful to him in his career. He sold his comfortable three-bedroom home on Long Island to rent an apartment in Manhattan, at an astronomical figure. The apart-

132

ment was tastefully but expensively decorated. This young man and his wife had frequent parties — with the "right" people invited every time. The best Scotch was served. Nothing was too good for the guests.

Naturally, considerable cost was involved. His moderate-level salary simply could not support his high-level spending. Something had to give. Before long he was up to his neck with the friendly but firm finance company. Monthly income did not quite meet monthly outgo. Still, the spending did not stop. He even borrowed money to take his family on a Caribbean cruise.

Eventually, of course, it became evident to all that this confused young man was in financial hot water. Needless to say, he did not develop a reputation for being the kind of manager who could be entrusted with important decisions involving the firm's money. His career, instead of moving ahead, was stopped cold. Why? Expensive "front." His high living had let him down . . . and not too easy.

Watch Your Boss . . . He's Watching You

This is an extreme example, but even less extreme cases can be damaging to a promising career. For example, an art dirctor bought a more luxurious car than his company president. Both he (the president) and his wife were baffled at how this particular employee could afford such a fine car. They were not envious — they were simply surprised at the lack of financial restraint shown by the artist. At first they were primarily concerned that he might get into financial trouble. Then, when further evidence of a lack of economy appeared, their concern grew into antagonism. Such a situation is not at all ideal for growing in stature within any company.

A former boss once said to me, "A man who cannot manage his own financial affairs cannot manage a firm's business affairs."

He had good reason to feel that way. Earlier in his career he had occasion to hire a man as general manager of one of his companies. The man made an excellent appearance. But soon after reporting for work, he was revealed to be in such financial difficulty that it was necessary for him to borrow to pay his income tax. Also, he was deep in debt for a full-house air-conditioner, plus a number of other major investments for his own and his family's comfort. Then, lo and behold, with debts piled all around him, he went out and bought his wife a brand new car — on credit, of course. At first, we all thought he had another source of income;

but it soon leaked out that he was spending money he hoped to earn some time in the future. But here's the big point: he was never able to pay for these things out of his earnings — at least, not from salary paid by our firm. You see, he just did not last very long in the job.

If you want to really understand why it is important to live within your means, then try to put yourself in the position of a big boss. Suppose you had an employee who was obviously enjoying luxuries beyond what was reasonable for his salary level. Then suppose you heard some rumors that this same person was getting deeper and deeper into debt. What would be your reaction? Chances are you'd say to yourself, "Better not let that boy get in a position to spend the company's money. He'll wreck us!"

Have A Nest Egg

Some firms go so far as to have stern policies on the subject of employee debts. Many automatically discharge a man (or woman) if they hear of a missed payment on an installment purchase. And it's hard to find a company that will honor a garnishee of salary. They simply say "good-bye" to the employee the minute the garnishee form is received.

So you can see that this business of financial management is quite important to your career. But, aside from career considerations, you should keep in mind that it's always good to have a little nest egg to tide you over, should something untoward happen to your income. Remember — you can have an extended illness. Your firm could be merged, with a resulting reduction in staff.

Do you remember the TV drama "Throw Me A Rope"? I'll never forget the torment portrayed in the face of the middle-level executive who lost his job because his firm was sold. While he did eventually get another job, it was a miracle that his meager funds held out long enough to re-establish himself. But what if he had had no funds at all? What if he had had debts instead of assets?

To Summarize

It is helpful to have a pleasant home and to entertain reasonably. But when this kind of socializing results in living beyond your means, it can mean only disaster for both you and your career.

Live comfortably, of course. Enjoy what luxuries you can afford. Entertain as often as seems appropriate, but not so often that your boss will begin to wonder where the money is coming from.

In short — live naturally, live comfortably, live as a sociable human being . . . but, above all, *live within your means.* Demonstrate that you know how to manage your own money, so that you may, some day, be entrusted with the management of other people's money. This is something you *must* begin demonstrating if you're to become head of your firm before forty.

21

USE PUBLICITY TASTEFULLY

In a recent television interview, an actress was asked, "Why did you have such a quick success and then drop out of popularity?" The interviewer was trying to establish the reason why a promising young starlet had failed to appear in a single movie for more than two years after having had three important successes during her very first year in Hollywood.

Her answer: "I thought I could reach the top through talent alone. I now know I made a big mistake when I shunned the 'arrangements' of publicity agents, and refused to be seen at the 'right places' with prominent young actors."

We like to think that ability alone will carry us to the top in any chosen field . . . whether it be acting or a business career. This book has made an attempt to show that many other factors are important to reaching a lofty goal. One of these factors is tasteful use of publicity.

Don't Go Overboard

Note that I say "tasteful." Too many eager-beavers think they are making progress whenever they get their names in the papers . . . no matter what circumstances surround the news item. This is an unfortunate use of a potentially valuable career tool.

To give an. extreme example . . . let's suppose a young man is photographed hanging by his legs from the George Washington Bridge with a package of his company's product gripped in his teeth. Without a doubt, he will draw a few reporters, along with the policemen who come to arrest him. Furthermore, it is almost a certainty that both he and his product will receive some publicity from the stunt.

But at what price?

Whenever people think of him and his product, they will associate them with an impression of a nutty exhibition of foolishness. This does not make for a favorable impression. The effect can only be harmful.

Taking a more realistic example . . . I know of an ethical drug firm that forbids the use of models (sometimes called hostesses or demonstrators) at trade conventions. The managers of this company are not prudes. They simply believe an ethical product should. not be connected with the razzle-dazzle and ballyhoo which is perfectly acceptable for some other classes of items.

Nevertheless, a certain amount of publicity is definitely helpful to you and to your firm. If you are careful to present your own and your company's profile to the public in a dignified manner, you will surely reap important rewards in the form of greater esteem for yourself and your products. Indeed, you owe it to your company as well as to your own career to have a program of planned public relations.

Different Types Of Publicity

Publicity is usually directed to two main groups. The first is the consuming public; the second, trade and industry.

General publicity to the consuming public is designed to create a favorable attitude toward your product, your company, and its executives. It paves the way for "harder-sell" advertising, which stimulates the urge to buy your product or your service. To be effective, this phase of publicity should be a continuing program. This usually means retaining a public relations firm which maintains a constant flow of information releases to the major news media.

Publicity to the trade is somewhat different. While its main goal again is the creation of a favorable attitude toward your company and its product, it can be a little more direct. News releases usually contain announcements of advertising appropriations, or investments in new plants and products. Sometimes a promotion of a key executive is sufficiently newsworthy to warrant a squib in trade journals. All of these releases boil down to some tactful bragging about the progress of your organization, but if done tastefully, they will have a favorable effect on customers and industry colleagues alike.

Toot Your Horn, A Little

Don't be afraid to use company's established department for the release of favorable publicity about yourself and the phase of the business for which you are responsible. If you receive a promotion, or if you are responsible for the promotion of someone else, it is perfectly acceptable for you to suggest a news release. If you institute a new promotion, or if you develop a new wrinkle for merchandising your product line, it will do both you and your organization a great deal of good to have this information appear in trade and consumer publications.

Then, there are more subtle ways to gain tasteful publicity. You may have a colleague suggest a speaking engagement and then issue a general release on the principle points of your speech. You may write articles of general interest, stressing points that can be helpful to the prestige of your company and yourself.

I know of a president of a large division of a proprietary products company who sponsors an annual study on supermarket merchandising of non-foods. He then prepares an expertly polished presentation which can be used at trade shows and conventions. This gives him and the public relations firm retained by the company an excellent opportunity to release interesting data to the trade at frequent intervals. Use of this material by publications is almost 100 percent, because it is substantially non-commercial in nature. The resulting prestige to this imaginative young man is perhaps one of the reasons he is the head of a division where many of his subordinates are considerably older and more experienced than he.

Timing Is Important

One of the big initial dangers in becoming conscious of the values of publicity is the possibility of poor timing in the release of news items. I remember the words of my ex-boss, Tom Huston. When asked why he did not approve a strong publicity project, he said: "We are not ready for it yet. We need to be sure of the soundness of our program before we announce it to the world."

How right he was! Perhaps you remember the barrage of publicity accorded the young man who founded a new radio network a few years ago. He was pictured as a boy genius, hopping planes from one city to another, signing contracts with station after station. What a let-down when only a few months later a news story told of the failure of his firm. In this case, the big publicity build-up had a boomerang effect. Instead of greater prestige, this lad became the object of pity and ridicule. It would have been far better for him to hold down the extravagant claims until he was certain that he would not have to eat the words of his own publicity agent.

In the questionnaire to outstanding young corporation presidents, previously mentioned, I asked these men to rate the relative importance of "planned public relations" to their own climbing up the executive ladder. They were asked to rate this factor as "important," "very important," or "not important." Three to one, it was rated "very important." Not a single respondent rated "planned public relations" as "unimportant" to his success.

Yes, publicity can help you in your climb to the top. But remember to use good judgment in timing as well as in the selection of subject matter. If you keep it tasteful, publicity will speed you toward your goal of company head before you're forty.

22

THE "IMPOSSIBLE" TAKES LONGER — BUT IT'S WORTH IT

One of the most important qualities of a sure-to-reach-the-top executive is his willingness to seek out the seemingly impossible problems and then work on them untiringly until they are solved. The case history of almost any top-flight businessman will support this view.

President At 30

Langbourne Williams, who became President of Freeport Sulphur Company at 30, was son of a well-to-do banker in Richmond, Virginia. After two years at Harvard Business School, young Williams made a European trip (and $1,000 for himself as organizer and guide of a tourist party), then worked for a New York bank before entering the family banking business.

He was called back to Richmond by the sudden illness of his father. He determined to get ahead fast in the Richmond bank, and figured the best way was to dig into a part of the bank's business which nobody else was paying much attention to. He hit upon Freeport Sulphur Company, in which the bank had a big interest. The deeper he dug, the more close-mouthed became the self-seeking officers of Freeport Sulphur . . . till Williams began a proxy fight to oust the management.

At 27 he became vice president and treasurer, at $20,000 a year. Three years later he was named head of the firm.

How? Why? Because he was not afraid to tackle a problem that looked tough, and was tough. And, because Langbourne Williams is the kind of man who likes a problem that seems impossible. He knows that the *impossible* problems take longer to solve . . . but when they are solved, they open doors that might otherwise require a lifetime of waiting.

Roadblocks Cleared

Many problems which appear to be unsolvable receive their "impossible" tag because the very people who must be depended upon to carry out the solution have personal reasons for not wanting to see the problem solved. Naturally, this puts an almost overwhelming roadblock in the path of any enterprising executive who is seeking a genuine solution.

I know a company president who found it possible to overcome just such a roadblock and, in the process, save his company from possible bankruptcy.

The company had suffered from a great deal of executive turnover. The root problem centered around a top-heavy administrative structure which resulted in a disproportionately high overhead. It got worse and worse, year after year . . . and one top executive after another was sacrificed because he could not seem to find the solution. Oh yes, one courageous general manager made a token move in the right direction. He cut the home office payroll by eleven people. But this was a mere drop in the bucket compared with the savings really needed to restore the firm to its rightful earning position.

Then the company elected a new president from within the ranks. Within six months he had completely reorganized the firm, and profits increased by nearly 70 percent. He closed one of the smaller plants, despite the indignant pleas of those of his subordinates who had various reasons for wanting to see it remain in operation. Then he combined several departments into one, and where the company formerly had three top-level financial men, he cut it to one head accountant. Tackling the work flow, he and his staff were able to improve procedures to the point where eighteen employees were doing the work formerly handled by forty-one. He made all department heads organize their staffs in such a way that they could accomplish everything the company needed with a smaller work force. He set up strict departmental budgets and made everyone stick to them.

In short . . . he reorganized the entire company along economy lines within the span of a few short months.

Why had he been able to accomplish what others had found impossible . . . and in a comparatively short period of time? It simply boils down to a willingness to accept a tough job and stay with it until the problem is licked — even in the face of opposition from people who are doing their best to inject the word "impossible" into the picture.

Tough Jobs At Every Level

While both of the above examples refer to corporation presidents, you should recognize that there are seemingly impossible situations at every level of business. What's more, most of them are just waiting for someone to come along and correct them.

Milestones of progress in almost any endeavor are found where somebody *did* what somebody else said *couldn't be done*. Napoleon said: " 'Impossible!' That's not good French!" A lot of promising people in business will get ahead faster when they drop the word from their English.

I cannot count the times I have heard these words: "It can't be done." I still hear those untrue words, every week. It seems that almost any time a tricky problem is up for discussion, there is someone in the room who thinks it's impossible. And most of the time that person is genuinely sincere in his hopelessness. This is just the time for a courageous young man to prove that even the impossible problems can be solved.

There is no better way to create an enthusiastic attitude toward yourself than by demonstrating an ability to solve knotty problems. More than likely your own superior is aware of a number of weak points within his department or division, but he has no one who wants the job of correcting them . . . no one who thinks he could correct those weak points. Just think of how grateful your superior would be to hear even one lonely voice cry out, "Let's try and see if something can be done about it."

To Be Big, THINK BIG

When you stop to think about all the "impossible" tasks that have been accomplished, it makes one wonder if there is anything that is truly beyond the realm of possibility.

Tom Huston, Chairman of the Board, and my boss when I became president of House of Huston, had a favorite saying. "If you will think big, you will act big. And if you act big, you will be big." He was speaking from personal experience, having built several fortunes from virtually nothing . . . nothing, that is, but courage, vision, and a conviction that anything can be accomplished if you believe in it and are willing to work for it.

Early in House of Huston's history we made a habit of doing the impossible. We had a network of some 100 representatives calling on the trade from coast to coast. Starting out with great enthusiasm, it soon developed that the sales volume could not possibly support such a large sales force. But, after spending two years of time and effort building up such a fine organization, we could not stand to see more than half of it go down the drain. And, worse still . . . we owed a debt to those faithful representatives who had given so generously of their loyalty to the company.

I remember discussing the problem with a colleague just prior to a management meeting which had been called to decide what to do with our sales personnel. We were in agreement that our field selling organization must be preserved, at any cost. But how could it be done without dragging the company down into bankruptcy? After an hour of discussion we had the answer. We would offer our sales force to other manufacturers, thereby spreading selling costs over a greater volume of sales. Within two weeks I was assigned the job of finding a couple of non-competing manufacturers in need of field sales help. Within two months our entire sales force was self-supporting . . . larger and more effectively perhaps than many that represented companies many times our size.

He Buys Trouble

I know a man who makes a career of buying trouble. His principle activity is financing firms which are floundering and need both financial and management guidance. The worse the balance sheet, the better he seems to like the company. Foolish, you say? . . . especially when he is putting his own money into the venture? Far from it. He says the real opportunities for satisfaction and personal gain are to be found in situations where the firm is in less than excellent shape. "I've never found a bargain," he has been heard to say, "by looking for a company that does not need help."

But his technique would be something less than successful if he did not have an unshakable faith in his ability to do the *impossible* or *near-impossible*. One time he bought an interest in a corporation that needed additional capital amounting to more than ten times his own investment in that firm. What's more . . . he knew, at the time he plunked down his own cash, that it needed this huge sum to survive and grow. But with courage, determination, and hard work, he immediately set out to interest others in the possibilities of the company. Furthermore, he spent considerable time on an analysis of past financial statements, and on the basis of his findings, suggested certain changes in policy. He set up budgets. He formalized both a short-range and a long-range plan. He helped infuse the executive group with renewed enthusiasm. He instituted tests of new products and new marketing programs.

Did it pay off? Within eighteen months the profit-and-loss statement showed such a complete reversal of operating results that it was possible to attract every penny required to put the company on its feet.

Ford's Challenge

The story is told of Henry Ford who, on at least one occasion, called in his engineers and asked them how much it was costing the Ford Motor Company to build a car. When the answer was given, he stated simply, "Well then, that's how much we will charge for our cars next year. Now it's up to you to find a way to make the car more economically so we can show a profit."

That's really going out on a limb. But without challenges like that during the early years of Ford's history, the automobile might never have sold at a price low enough to encourage the mass purchasing that was vital to modern assembly-line production techniques.

Motto For You: "Can Do"

Next time somebody tells you "it can't be done," immediately reverse that view — in your own mind, at least. Then work out a way to accomplish that "impossible" aim. You'll find the experience immensely rewarding.

Adopt this kind of positivism toward seemingly impossible situations, and you'll demonstrate to yourself and to others that you have one of the qualities essential to a corporation president.

Cultivate this kind of positive, "can do," thinking.

Make it a habit.

It will help speed you to a corporation presidency before you're forty.

23

IF YOUR NAG LAGS, CHANGE FEED BAGS

This chapter will be short. Its message is necessarily brief . . . and somewhat unpleasant, to boot.

That mixed-up metaphor in the chapter title suggests some further metaphorical observations:

"Don't change horses in midstream," you've been told . . . but unless your horse gives fair promise of getting you to shore (your goal), you've no choice but to tag another nag — one that's going your way, of course — and climb on, as far up front as you can.

"A rolling stone gathers no moss" . . . but unless you can keep rolling along at a fair rate of progress in your present firm, it may be time to think about gathering in more "long green" somewhere else.

If you "accepted a promising position" with your company some time ago and you're still getting little more than promises, maybe you're no longer in the race. Don't wait around till they put you out to pasture. Maybe now's the time to take a good close look at yourself and your company.

Do Your Best . . .
But Don't Leave The Rest
To "Whatever Tomorrow May Bring"

Yes . . . in spite of all your planning and preparation . . . in spite of all your ambition and willingness to work . . . despite the fact that you are obviously qualified for bigger jobs in your company — even though you have faithfully given attention to all those things that should move you upward on the executive ladder, it may develop that you are not making the progress you should.

If this happens, it can be due to only one of two reasons:

(1) There is somthing wrong with you.
(2) There is something wrong with your company.

If and when you reach this point in your own career, the first thing you should do is *search your own conscience.* See if you have lived up to all the requirements for a man who wants to succeed in business. Be honest with yourself. Don't gloss over your own failures or the inadequacies of your personality. If you find something wrong, start all over again and correct the errors you've been making.

(There is a sort of philosophical attitude which says: "I have done my best today; now I must be content with whatever tomorrow may bring." That philosophy is quite all right for a lot of people — perhaps for most people — but it is not all right for you. If you are going to climb to the top in business, and stay there, you'll have to do your best every day and never be satisfied with what tomorrow brings. For you, the approach of contentment will signal the ending of progress . . . and you must make certain that day is far distant.)

So, first take a good look at yourself. Maybe that's where the trouble lies, and that's where you'll take corrective measures. But if, after critical self-analysis, you are convinced that you have lived by most of the rules and are trying honestly to improve in those areas where you have fallen somewhat short of perfection, then it is well for you to turn your analytical eye on the firm for which you work.

Is the company unappreciative of outstanding effort and performance? Do they prefer to reward on the basis of cronyism rather than ability? Is the firm controlled by one family and do the relatives get all the best jobs? Do they prefer to pay as little as possible for executive jobs rather than reward those who are responsible for improving profits?

If all or most of these things are true (and I must state here that this is rarely the case) then you have been unfortunate enough to become associated with a company that cannot possibly be your vehicle to a successful career. If you should genuinely come to this conclusion, then you have no choice but to change firms.

Read The Writing On The Wall

Without mentioning any names, it is well known that a certain young man saved and put on the road to greatness, a company that was floundering on the edge of extinction. He came up with a dramatic idea for shifting the firm's emphasis to a new field with an entirely different concept. After a few years, during which the business grew and prospered, the young man was made executive vice president. But then the president's son was graduated from college. Soon friction developed and eventually it was made known that the next president would be the son rather than the brilliant young vice president who had literally "made over" the firm.

After the writing was on the wall, it became obvious that the best thing was for him to seek another connection. He secured a vice presidency with a canned foods firm, the largest in its field, and in a few years was made president.

In this instance, the promising young man recognized the futility of trying to adjust to an impossible situation. He did the only thing possible. He moved to another company, where his talent and energy could be, and were, recognized and rewarded.

Be Sure You Are Right

So, my advice to you . . . if you want to make career progress without undue delay . . . be sure you are in the right firm. But remember, it is far easier to err on the side of being over-critical than it is to have a complete understanding of your own value and contribution to your company. Do not act hastily. But once you are sure, you can do your career no greater favor than to move on to a firm where you will have a better opportunity to achieve your goal of becoming head of your firm before forty.

24

ALWAYS ACT LIKE A PRESIDENT . . .
Even Though, At Present, You're Far From The Top

How often have you heard, "The bigger the man, the nicer the guy"?

That's just another way of saying that a leader in any field has certain qualities that make him immediately stand out. In this regard, business is no different from any other field.

There are exceptions to every rule. There always will be. It is generally true, as we saw in Chapter 16, that the chief executive of a firm is genuinely liked and admired by more employees than almost any other person in the company. (We all chuckle at Cartoonist Jimmy Hatlo's "Mr. Bigdome," Cartoonist Chic Young's "Mr. Dithers," and other popular caricatures of the boss; but people in business, and especially in big business, know that *these* are the exceptions.)

It is often obvious that qualities of congeniality which make a chief executive genuinely liked by his subordinates are the same qualities which play a large role in helping him to achieve the presidency.

Study the ranking officer in your company — if you are now employed in commerce. Note the qualities which make him the personality he must be to exercise leadership over so many people of varying interests, abilities and inclinations. You'll no doubt conclude that:

   . . . he has a well-developed ability to get along with and to stimulate his subordinates;

   . . . he knows how to put people at ease;

   . . . he gets to the point quickly;

   . . . he's fast at grasping facts.

However, he nearly always accomplishes all this without flustering anybody, and certainly without making others feel inferior.

Really Big Bosses Seldom Act Bossy

I was House of Huston's president when the corporation was acquired by Sterling Drug, Inc., a big corporation with numerous subsidiaries and divisions. Naturally, some of the policies which were all right for our firm before it was acquired by Sterling, were somewhat different from those of the new parent company. Certain changes had to be made.

Not once, in my conferences with the Chairman of the Board or with the President of this huge corporation, did I ever get the impression that they were critical of our previous practices. They seemed to go out of their way to emphasize that these changes had to be made for purposes of uniformity and not just because they believed that their policies were better than ours had been.

In several instances, of course, I knew full well that they had procedures and policies that were far superior to those we had been using. But neither of these big business men (both of whom were drawing salaries in six figures) made any attempt to demonstrate superiority over me or any of our corporate officers . . . even though our company was less than one-fifth the size of the organization they were managing.

Once I met with the Chairman of the Board to discuss our accounting system. He said simply, "I've been looking over your accounting set-up, and it appears to be very good. In some ways it may be better than ours. But since we must have uniformity for purposes of financial statement consolidation, I'm afraid you'll have to change to our system." Then, with a chuckle, he said, "Maybe it would be better if we changed to your system, but that would be the tail wagging the dog."

Meet People On Their Own Level

Most big executives, I believe, know how to be "one of the boys" without losing any of their dignity . . . and it should be remembered, always, that a certain amount of dignity is attached to the *office* of president, even though the *person* who is president may not be at all inclined to dignity. But, back to the point:

Most big executives seem to have an unusual capacity for meeting people on their own level without damaging the respect which every subordinate must feel for his boss. Recall how American Writing Paper's President, Sidney Willson, talked with the veteran paper-mill employee? (Chapter 12.) A good executive can, in the course, of a single day, modify his personality so completely that he appears to be at ease with any kind of employee . . . from truck driver to research chemist. He seems to have a way of speaking their language, no matter where he happens to be. But in every case, his people know that, even though he is a great guy, he is still the big boss. They like him as boss because he is a great guy . . . they'd like him as a great guy even though he were not boss.

It has been said that a person who has the qualities necessary for top responsibility stands out from the crowd like a peach atop a basket of grapes. People recognize leadership ability long before the authority is made official. If this be true, then why not start acting like a corporation president right now . . . no matter what your present job happens to be.

Be A Big Nut

Ralph Parlette, well-known inspirational lecturer of some years ago, had a famous story which may serve to illustrate my point.

"The world is made up of two kinds of people," said Parlette (in essence), holding up a glass jar filled with a lot of little dry beans and a few big walnuts.

"Most of us are just average, ordinary people," he would continue, pointing to the beans. "See all those little beans in the jar? Let's say the little beans are most of us . . . just everyday people, getting along the best way they can.

"But, look! This world inside our glass jar isn't just made up of little beans. Here are a few big walnuts in here, see? Yes, there are some big nuts in our world . . . just as there are a few big nuts here in our glass jar.

"Now, notice that the big nuts are not all on the bottom, where you'd expect them to be since they're heavier. They're not all on the top, either. They're all in among the little beans . . . some near the bottom, some in the middle, some near the top.

"But, see what happens when I shake the jar. I look under the jar here at the bottom, and I don't see those big nuts that were there on the bottom before I shook it. I still see those big ones up at the top, though. Let's shake the jar again; real hard this time.

"There! See those big nuts moving up? Yes, that's what happens every time I shake the jar. The little beans just jostle around among themselves, but those big nuts manage to get a little higher in the jar every time I shake it up . . . just like the "big nuts'" in our human world get nearer and nearer the top with every shake-up. They rise inevitably — almost automatically — because they're bigger than the little beans around them."

The metaphor is obvious . . . the conclusion, clear: *If you want to get up in this world, don't be a little bean.*

It's important to *Think Big* so you may become *BIG,* as we shall see in Chapter 26.

You can build a reputation for leadership and enthusiastic dignity long before you have to worry about the responsibilities of a high-level position. The fact that you do not have these stagger-ing responsibilities will give you more time to concentrate on your own personality. Then, you will be ready with the right kind of well-rounded personality when the big day comes that you are tapped for the big job.

And, still more important . . . the very fact that you are work-ing on it will help speed the day when you will be recognized as a man with top management talent.

Not So Easy As It Sounds

But don't get the idea that's quite as easy as it sounds. It isn't.

Adopting the demeanor of a head-of-the-firm usually means developing an outlook that is far different from that of associates with whom you are in daily contact. Many times, your co-workers will think and talk about the company from their own personal points of view. You will have to start thinking about the company as if it were your own personal responsibility, and one of the most important things in your life. In short, you will have to become more company-minded than anyone you know . . . except possibly the president of your company, himself.

You'll know you have at least begun to approach a degree of company-mindedness when your friends start griping about some company policy and you consciously refuse to join in . . . even if it's only good-natured spoofing. You'll know that your dignity as a potential head of the firm will not be enhanced by anything but a positive attitude toward your firm.

A sense of humor is a very valuable asset, in business as else-where. However, if your humor has to be built around sarcasm toward your company or your superiors, then you simply are not growing in the direction of your ultimate goal of top-level respon-sibility.

I once heard a remark from a talented young middle-level executive. Perhaps as a means of gaining some attention or perhaps because he simply wanted to be funny, he made the following remark to a gathering of new sales trainees: "We have just one policy around here. On Monday we make a lot of fast decisions, and then we spend the rest of the week changing them."

Of course, he received a roar from the group. But the price of that laughter was beyond measure. It left every member of that meeting with a little question in his mind about the soundness of the company's decisions. Such actions on the part of a man with presidential aspirations are unthinkable.

Sure, make jokes . . . but if they must involve a company, make them up about a competitor.

To Summarize

Start acting like a president, even though your goal of being head of the firm is just a dream.

Impossible?

No.

What I mean is: *Cultivate such presidential attributes as company-mindedness, appropriate dignity without stuffiness, gentlemanly consideration for others, directness without rudeness, quick grasping of facts; directing, instructing, controlling, regulating, administering, authorizing, leading, enthusing, inspiring — but strive always to do these things without separating yourself from those around you . . . below, above, and on either side.*

Then, you'll be acting like the company head you expect to be before you're forty.

25

LEARN TO REMEMBER NAMES AND FACES

The human mind is perhaps the most intricate, baffling, and wonderful of all creations. Untrained, it produces wasted lives. Rightly disciplined and uprighted directed, it yields life's greatest satisfaction — material, mental, spiritual.

Memory, the Filing Department of the mind, is like a bank. You can't draw anything out until you've put something in. In no phase of business does memory serve us better than in recalling names and faces.

Archbishop Ryan was walking along a Baltimore street one day when he was stopped by a man who apparently attended church at least once in a while. He knew the Archbishop's face, but couldn't place it. "Now where in hell have I seen you?" he asked perplexedly. "From where in hell do you come, sir?" retorted the clergyman, with a twinkle.

Work At It

Whether you come from Helena or Harrisburg, one of the essentials to sure progress up the exectuive ladder is the ability to remember names and faces. It's something you'll have to work on, unless you're different from the rest of us. Most people — top executives included — have a difficult time remembering names and faces. You most certainly will make your climb to the top a great deal smoother by developing this helpful ability.

"I just can't remember names." When was the last time you heard that from one of your business associates? When did you say it last? Probably not long ago. You may think you have absolutely no talent for retaining names. Your mind may seem to be a sieve when it comes to remembering names and faces of people you meet.

If so, there's a reason. If you don't remember names and faces, it's not because you *can't.*

Remembering names and faces is something *you* can develop. Few business men have climbed the ladder of success without developing that highly-important faculty.

As a matter of fact, most people who show an astounding ability at reembering names and faces actually have no better memory than you. The difference is they have trained theirs through hard work, and by adopting one of the association systems advocated by so-called memory experts.

Farley's Famous Memory

James A. Farley made himself famous and contributed greatly to the election successes of Franklin D. Roosevelt by remembering names. In his 1932 tour on behalf of the Democratic candidate, Farley met thousands upon thousands of citizens. It has been said that he remembered almost every name, and later wrote personal letters to many thousands of these hand-shake supporters, asking for their continuing active effort on behalf of Roosevelt. The result is recorded on an important page of American history.

Everyone likes to feel he is important. You do. I do. And every employee in any business or industrial organization *is* important. If he is not important, then he is surplus and should be released from the payroll. The best way you can show a person you recognize his importance is to take the trouble to learn his name. It's that simple, and easy.

Schwab Knew Every Employee

Charles M. Schwab, who later became head of U. S. Steel, once knew the names of all eight thousand employees in a mill he managed. That's what the record shows. Even many years later, on a visit to this same mill, he was able to name 500 of the 800 employees remaining from the original 8,000.

The amazing memory of a Charlie Schwab or a Jim Farley is not absolutely essential to a successful career in business. Indeed, it is not likely that anyone will expect you to remember the names and faces of 8,000 employees. But you'll certainly have to do better than the many otherwise capable executives who don't take the trouble to learn even the names of all the key people in their organizations. Since this laxity is so prevalent in business today, it gives you an outstanding opportunity to stand out as a man of rare qualities. All you have to do is to develop this ability to a reasonable degree.

Some Tricks To Make It Easy

There are a few tricks you can use quite effectively in developing your ability to remember names and faces.

First, and perhaps the most important, of these memory tools is to *care enough* to remember. The big secret of a good memory is attention. An ancient sage with the heart of a poet (Whose name somebody forgot to record) once said: "Memory is the daughter of attention and the mother of knowledge."

One of the main reasons you forget a name is that you never really learned it in the first place. You didn't *pay* attention, so you didn't *get* retention. This idea of motivation is more important than you realize in the business of remembering names and faces.

For many years, I marvelled at my wife's unusual ability to remember names of authors and plays. To make it even more mysterious, she remembered these facts about many theatrical productions we had never seen. Then suddenly one day I realized that I too had a large store of information about some things in which I had no personal contact. I could remember the names of executives and the sales volumes of numerous corporations. Where had I picked up this data? The same place my wife had acquired her knowledge of authors and plays: from newspapers and magazines. I was simply motivated to remember the things which were most interesting to me, and my wife remembered the things that most interested her.

First Names And Nicknames

The tendency to use first names of business associates seems to be growing. Occasionally you find a corporation president (like a New Englander I once worked under) who insists on being addressed as "Mister," but more and more heads of firms, it seems, like to be addressed by their first names . . . at least by major executives.

Tom Huston (who founded Tom Huston Peanut Company and became a millionnaire before 30; then founded another corporation, House of Huston, and made another tidy fortune) has always been "Tom" to his executives, some of whom were several decades younger than he. In my years of association with him, I never sensed any lack of respect on the part of younger executives who always addressed him as "Tom." He was never unavailable to any employee, and I am sure he enjoyed greater admiration and esteem throughout the organization because he did not set himself up as "Mr. Big."

The office of president carries its own weight when it comes to authority, respect, and such things; and I believe it is quite unnecessary to attempt to add to that weight by insisting that the head of the firm be "Mr. Big." I believe that the corporation president can get closer to his subordinates and do a more effective job of leadership when he is generally addressed by his first name, by major executives anyway. Of course, this means signing a lot of letters with his first name only.

As a rule, I supose it's no harder to remember first names than surnames; but in a large organization there are likely to be so many Jims, Johns, and Bills that something other than first names helps in remembering as well as for day-to-day identification. In such cases, nicknames seem justified . . . so long as the nicknamed person does not object. In fact, I suppose any nickname is in order so long as it pleases the nicknamed. Obvious nicknames to be avoided, of course, are those making reference to physical characteristics — such as "Curly" for the bald-headed bookkeeper or "Slim" for the rotund researcher.

Best of all nicknames, of course, is one which the subject has given himself.

When I lived in Miami, one of my good friends and business associates was the gifted artist-designer, Martin Dawson, whose home was in a preferred residential section called Coconut Grove. Being near salt (and softly-moonlit) waters of beautiful Biscayne Bay, the community is visited now and then by more-or-less uninvited creatures, including the ungainly landcrab. This irrelevant but inescapable fact led Dawson to nail over the doorway to his workshop-studio a shingle with the self-bestowed title, "Baron of Landcrab Gulch." Soon Artist Dawson was known, throughout the company and throughout the community, as "The Baron." He tells me he occasionally receives mail addressed merely to "The Baron of Landcrab Gulch." In such a case, an intentionally bizarre nickname helps many people remember the man and his name.

Whenever an acquaintance has a well-known nickname, knowing it will help you remember that person . . . whether you address him by his nickname or keep your intercourse more formal.

Avoid Embarrassment

One way to assist your motivation to remember names and faces is to picture in your mind the embarrassment of forgetting the name at some future meeting. All of us have gone through this painful experience. In business it can be downright catastrophic. Here's a true story told on himself by a friend of mine:

In the early part of World War II, he was named administrator of his father's estate. One day he was stopped on the street by a man with a familiar face. "I believe I owed your Dad a little money when he died," said the face whose name my friend could not recall. "I'll have a look at the books, and let you know," replied my friend, thinking he knew the man's name — but not sure enough to call him by name, and too embarrassed to uncover his uncertainty. My friend decided that this man was somebody else, and a few days later wrote a note to this other, mistakenly-identified, man . . . telling him that the estate records showed nothing outstanding against him. Then, a day or two later, my friend saw in the local paper a picture of the man he had encountered on the street, with information that he had been inducted and assigned to military duty at a distant point. Before my friend could get a mailing address and follow up on the matter, and advise the man that there *was* a balance of somewhat more than $100 due the estate, the man had been killed in action. Under the circumstances, my friend wrote off the amount due . . . not a great deal, but something which would have been paid had he connected the man's name and face when they met on the street.

Just as a model's face and figure *are* her fortune, so it figures that the face you don't remember can affect your fortune, in a case like that of my friend. You probably know of instances where such embarrassment was much more costly.

Don't Lose Cash By Forgetting The Face

You, too, can lose money by not remembering names and faces. And it can be quite embarrassing in other than monetary ways. It can lose friends, and customers.

When you meet a person for the first time, you must concentrate on the name, asking him to repeat it if you miss it or fail to hear it distinctly. If the name is unusual, ask how it is spelled. You won't offend the person or make a fool of yourself. Chances are the person will be flattered that you really want to make a point of knowing him . . . and there's more than a good chance that *he'll* remember *you* better for it.

After you're sure you have the name correct in your own mind, pound it home by repeating it as often as possible, as soon as possible . . . especially while you're talking with the person in that first conversation. Use his name at the end of every sentence, as you talk with him. Begin your remarks by addressing him by name. As you repeat his name, over and over in that conversation, you'll be fastening it more and more securely in your memory.

Bizarre Association

You'll find yourself remembering names of customers and co-workers if you cultivate the habit of associating each name with something else. A related fact, an impression, a picture . . . it doesn't matter what you choose for this mental association. The more bizarre, the more likely you are to remember both the association and the name.

If a man's name is Horn, you might associate it with a blaring automobile, careening down a street and crashing into a music store loaded with French horns. Or, if he has the appropriate personality, you may want to picture him with a couple of red horns sticking out of his head. But be sure to associate the name with so many ideas, facts, and pictures that you simply cannot forget it. Then recall these pictures and facts to your mind as frequently as possible. You'll be amazed how long the entire group of images will remain with you.

Memory Makes Friends

Yes, it takes a little effort and patience. But you will be repaid many times over for the effort, in warm personal relationships with both your superiors and your subordinates. You'll make more friends, more easily . . . and, as Francis Bacon wrote, "without friends the world is but a wilderness."

If you fail to remember a man's name, you are stating all too plainly that he did not make enough of an impression on you to encourage you to remember him. A man can forgive you many things, but he can never really forgive you the crime of not taking him seriously. So don't antagonize people by admitting that they are unimportant to you; don't admit it to yourself, for everybody *is* important to you, at least potentially.

No Substitute

You may think you can develop other abilities which will substitute for this ability to remember names and faces. There is no substitute.

When I was sales manager, I had on the team a salesman who recognized the importance of knowing names, but he simply would not put his mind to work and develop a system for anchoring his customers' names in his memory. He decided, instead, to maintain a little black book with the names of his customers in it. He referred to the book before each sales call.

One day he was at a convention with the president of our company. One by one, his top accounts approached our booth and he was unable to make a proper introduction . . . all because he had not related the names of his customers with their faces. Needless to say, he lost prestige in the eyes of his customers and his boss.

Remember . . . And You'll Be Remembered

It takes many qualities to earn a top corporation job at an early age. Not only must you have qualities way above the average, but you must know how to dramatize those qualities. I know of no better way to dramatize the uniqueness of your talents than by developing a better-than-average memory for names and faces. If you have not already acquired this ability, start cultivating it now. Investment in a memory course can pay big dividends. But even if you can't go that far, you can make a start in the right direction by developing a habit of concentrating on the names and faces of all new acquaintances and hammering them into your memory by repetition and association.

It is more than likely that before you are forty you will know hundreds of customers and fellow employees by faces and first names . . . that is, if you're to be anywhere near a corporation presidency before you're forty.

26

THINK BIG AND YOU'LL BE BIG

An ancient truism which will never grow old: "As a man thinketh in his heart, so is he."

This old saying will never be out of date because *thought is a renewing experience.* Correct thinking helps us keep young and vital, even though our thinking be thoroughly mature. Right thinking must always precede right action, and right action is the only sure way to achieve any worthy aim. It follows that right thinking plus right acting will assure success. Thinking *big* is thinking *right* if the bigness toward which thought proceeds amounts to benefits greater than the cost.

So, before you become big, you *must* think big.

Christopher Morley once wrote that "big shots are only little shots who keep on shooting." You must keep on shooting for bigger and bigger goals, if you're to achieve your goal of a corporation presidency before you're forty.

On your way to that goal, your most purposeful thinking takes the form of *sound planning* . . . the thing this book is all about.

Make no little plans for yourself. John Wanamaker (who was born to poverty but raised himself to the place of merchant prince) said: "Hardly any business man is half what he might be." Are you already planning to be more than half the success you *can* be? Planning is the first essential step, after thinking . . . or, as a part of your thinking.

Yes . . . *think big, and plan big . . .and you'll be big.*

Thinking Big Takes Courage

Nearly everybody I know wants to improve his position. Practically everyone would like to succeed better on the job. The average person wants to be promoted. Or, if he is self-employed, he'd like to do his work better, build up a greater demand for his product or services, and reap a larger income. Few people are satisfied with the results of their efforts. Most ambitious people crave the satisfaction of a sense of real success in what they undertake . . . and for most people that sense of real success is an elusive thing, a goal that's over the next hill, or the next one after that.

Why do some people achieve spectacular success in their careers while others bog down in mediocrity? Too often the difference is not in intelligence or a capacity for hard work. I have seen brilliant men passed over for promotion while a man of lower intellectual capacity was given the job. I have seen men (and women) who could hardly read or write, build big firms of their own and then go on to hire people with college degrees, at salaries less than a fraction of their own.

Invariably, these people who enjoy outstanding success have one big thing in common: they have the courage to *think big*.

How many times have you heard the story of a man who builds a fortune and loses it, only to build another one again at a later date. Surely this cannot be attributed to luck; one person could not be that lucky so many times in his life span. The answer lies in a mental attitude. They *think big* so they can *grow big*.

First Steps To Bigness

Thinking big means to condition your mind to the conviction that you can achieve a desired success far beyond that of the average person. It means picturing yourself making steady progress toward your goal, never doubting that you will make the grade with a reasonable amount of luck and a great amount of hard work. It means planning every move forward so you will not get side-tracked from your ultimate objective.

In short, *thinking big* is the first step toward *being big*.

Early in my career I went to work for a firm that started out with an initial capitalization of $25,000. Ten years later the company was sold for enough money to make millionaires of the family that had made the initial investment. Sound fantastic? Not when you consider that the $25,000 was but a small part of the investment made by the originators of the business. The most significant investment, quite probably, was the investment in courage and determination on the part of people who dared to *think big*.

I remember vividly those early days when we hardly knew whether our checks would be honored by the bank. In spite of many and frequent reverses, and in spite of little or no profit for several years running, the managers of that firm never ceased to think big and act big. They never questioned or doubted the ability of the company to grow until it was one of the leaders in its field. Needless to say, it was not too many years before all of its competitors were taking a long, hard look to see why this recent upstart was taking so much of their business.

No Mystery

There is no mystery in the so-called "magic" of thinking big. It is a necessary ingredient in the Formula of Success, simply because it sets a goal and keeps you on the track during your long journey toward that goal.

Every career is loaded with seemingly attractive opportunities which can distract and side-track if you are not careful to maintain a steady eye on the big objective that will give you ultimate satisfaction. As a matter of fact, it probably can be said that few great accomplishments have been achieved without a vision of a magnificent future on the part of some person with the talent for dressing and then doing something about it. A wishy-washy attitude toward your goal will always result in hit-or-miss progress. And that's no way to become head of your firm before forty.

Don't ever forget that *success and fickleness do not go together* . . . you've got to "keep on shooting" toward that goal you set for yourself back there at the beginning.

Thinking Big Brings Good Ideas

Thinking big will open the door to another secret for getting ahead in business . . . the capacity to think up ideas to help you and your firm move forward in the competitive struggle.

It has been said that there is never a shortage of jobs for a person with ideas. James D. Woolf, in a *Forbes* Magazine article, "Ideas Get the Job," tells of a lesson he learned as a boy. Anxious to earn extra money, he asked all three drug stores in his town for a job . . . any kind of a job. There were no openings. But a week later he found that one of the stores had taken on a new boy. Screwing up his courage, he asked the owner why.

"Well, I'll tell you, son," answered the druggist. "I didn't *think* I had a job open when you asked for one. But then Freddie came in with an idea. He owns a bicycle, and he suggested that I start a delivery service, meaning himself. That's a new notion for this town, and it's going to make a hit."

The main reason people never get into the habit of thinking big is that they are afraid of failure. Tom Huston, founder of several multi-million dollar firms, once told me: "John, if people only knew how many things I have tried that did not succeed. The reason for some of these successes is simply that I tried out a great number of ideas. Some of them *had* to work."

In a similar vein, I remember one of my early business associates who had created quite a reputation for creative thinking in the marketing field. (He is now executive vice president of a very large company, but at that time he was a brand merchandising manager.) His technique was to test every conceivable notion that popped into his head . . . providing it offered some hope of adding to the sale of his product line. Many of his ideas did not prove out upon small-scale testing. But whenever one did . . . which frequently happened . . . he quickly expanded it to a national promotion with fantastic results in the sale of his products. While other brand merchandising managers were handling perhaps two or three promotions each year, he was testing fifteen or twenty, from which he selected perhaps the top half-dozen for national distribution. Invariably, the law of averages resulted in his promotions yielding higher sales increases. Not only did he have more of them, but his active imagination gave him more promotions to choose from after careful testing.

He had mastered the art of thinking big. He wanted his brands to reach the top and then stay there. The only way he was sure this could be done was by thinking his way to the top.

Get Acquainted With Big Ideas

You'll go a long way in the direction of thinking big if you make it a habit to keep on the lookout for successful ideas of others. Your ideas need only be original in their application to your specific work of industry. Advertisements in your local newspapers will show you some new angles. Trade journals and even the classified telephone directory will give you ideas with a novel twist. They are full of better ways of doing things, and they will furnish a fertile field for imagination and initiative.

There is a saying that "anything man can conceive, he can achieve." Not only is this just as true today as it was a couple of generations ago, but today's miracles of science, including atomic power and even space flight, bear witness to the power of thinking big. How many people, with the exception of the Wright Brothers themselves, had the vision to believe that within a few score years of man's first flight in a heavier-than-air machine, it would become commonplace for people to have breakfast in New York and lunch in Los Angeles. Captain Eddie Rickenbacker shared that vision and because of his strong conviction, he was willing to resign a comfortable position with General Motors to take his chances on the weak and staggering young airline known as Eastern. The success of Eastern Airlines is just one more evidence of how success — both financial and personal achievement — can come to someone with a big dream who is willing to do something about it.

A Word Of Caution

Thinking big does not mean thinking haphazardly. It does not mean mere musing, or woolgathering. Thinking big *does* include thinking thoroughly, with a measure of maturity. Thinking big means starting your thinking on a solid foundation of facts.

Kenneth Keyes, Jr., in his excellent volume, *How To Develop Your Thinking Ability,* says: "We protect ourselves from facing facts by cleverly twisting our thinking . . . this twisting is called 'rationalization.' " He goes on to point out that correct thinking includes "separating the wisdom of the past from the out-of-date ideas, prejudices, humbugs, and bunk that accumulate . . . one of the toughest and yet one of the most important things we must do . . . The better we do this job of keeping our knowledge up-to-date, the more successful and the happier we will be."

In thinking big, don't let *wishful thinking* take the place of *purposeful thinking.* Don't mistake *fuzzy thinking* for *thinking big.*

To start *thinking big, know that nothing is impossible* . . . as we pointed out in Chapter 22.

In thinking big, and thinking yourself toward bigness, be careful not to become too big to be helpful. L. E. Frailey, in his witty little book titled *This Way Up,* points out that "little people in business think that 'helping out' will lose them the respect of people working under their supervision." The reverse is true, as a rule. You don't have to be bossy to be a good boss. Remember American Writing Paper Company's President Sidney L. Willson's statement to one of his workers: "If I can't help you and the other fellows here in the mill, I'll be falling down on my job."

Your job as president will be not merely to "make the other fellow work" (as Donald Nelson, Chairman of the War Production Board during World War II, once characterized his job); but to help everybody in your company do a better job, all down the line, by providing the spark, the inspiration, to more productive effort.

When you get to the top, you'll be in a position to think big because you'll have the over-all picture of your firm's operation. But don't wait till you get to the top to start thinking big, or you'll never become president.

Every Problem Has An Answer

Everyone has a few stock sayings which he uses freely whenever the occasion arises. I have at least one such saying, which by now my associates are undoubtedly tired of hearing. But I'm so completely convinced of its power to change things dramatically for the better that I simply must repeat it here:

> *Every problem has an answer. It is up to us to think our way to its solution.*

Sounds obvious, you say. Well then, why do companies fail, and why do people lose their jobs after a reversal in the trend of their firm's business? In my opinion, it's because someone has lost faith in his ability to think a problem through to a satisfactory solution. And, the bigger the problem, the bigger he'll have to think.

It never hurts to let your imagination run wild whenever you have a particularly perplexing problem. (This is not haphazard thinking; but broad, exploratory thinking.) You can sort the good ideas from the bad ones later. But the problems that most often seem to defy solution can usually be solved with a dramatically new or sometimes even a radical approach. Believe it or not, many of the nation's largest firms would not be in business today were it not for some radical thinking on the part of somebody among those firms' leaders. After all, the very nature of big business makes it inevitable that certain products or services will always be on a downgrade. The only way to overcome this loss, and to drive ahead to new heights, is by coming up with dramatic new ideas which often bring a firm into entirely new fields. That's why one of the popular axioms of modern business is: "You must always push ahead or you'll surely start falling behind."

Look Ahead, Look Up, Look Out

Many people cannot understand why firms are willing to spend 8, 9, or even 10 percent of their sales on research. In some cases, this is as much as or more than the firm's net profit. But the reason is a good one. The managements of these forward-looking companies are thinking ahead to a big future.

What is the main difference between a person who can be described as a "Big Man" and another who is not quite so big? Many times it can be traced directly to his ability to think big. He can imagine himself and his associates moving ahead steadily until they reach a goal that a man of lesser vision never dares to associate with himself. Perhaps it is because of a false sense of modesty, or perhaps it is because our educators do not stress the great potential for personal growth, but all too often our bright young businessmen fail to associate themselves personally with the triumphs of the future. They know that progress will be made and they know that they will be part of that progress. But too seldom do they seem to thrill to the realization that they may, through diligence and thinking big, have an opportunity to lead these conquests from a position at or near the top. Indeed, some of them are even afraid to talk the language of bigness, feeling, perhaps, that they will be accused of trying to put on airs.

I was invited to dinner by an old school chum. It was soon after a company I was associated with was sold. Naturally, he heard of my company changing hands, and he asked me a question or two. I answered his questions and, thinking he was genuinely interested, I began to elaborate on some of the behind-the-scenes details (avoiding confidential data, of course). To my astonishment, his face revealed not only a lack of understanding, but I could see that it made him uncomfortable to be talking about a subject which went beyond the everyday operation of a business. And, the most surprising thing of all is that the subject matter of this brief conversation can be found described in great detail in any first-year textbook on Business Organization. I finally concluded that this man, bright as he was, considered the subject of mergers and stock exchanges as something for the sole attention of business moguls who live and breathe in a world entirely apart from his own. In short, he did not, and, so far as I know, still does not, consider himself a candidate for the upper echelons of business management.

Always Think Big

But, since you are taking the time to read this book, and since you have set a goal to become head of your firm by forty, I feel confident that you are not making the mistake of failing to think big. But remember, always, even as you approach the pinnacle of your success, there will always be a temptation to think in a way other than big. Moreover, you may be surrounded by men who would prefer to see you more conservative in your thinking and planning. It won't be easy to look beyond into the distant future where success to you will mean that you must carry many, many others on your shoulders. But the rewards are tremendous, and the satisfaction is sweet for any man who dares to face ahead and say, "This great thing can be done if I believe in it enough and if I work to make it come true."

I hope you will be enjoying those rewards and tasting those sweet satisfactions, as head of your firm, before you're forty.

27

DO NOT STOP WHEN YOU REACH THE TOP
(or you may be through ... sort of impromptu)

Among the sages of the ages, whose thoughts have been preserved, I've found none who spoke more trenchantly in favor of the businessman advancing toward forty than did Francis Bacon when he said:

> Men of age object too much, consult too long, adventure too little, repent too soon, and seldom drive business home to the full period, but content themselves with a mediocrity of success.

Logic, proceeding from Sir Francis' observation, says that the man who becomes head of his firm *before* forty has that much better chance of enjoying something much greater than "mediocrity of success." The odds favor his going farther, faster.

"A good start is half the race." A start that's early, as well as good, will put you out in front and keep you ahead all the way to the finish.

Whether you're already off and running, or whether you're just beginning to plan your career, now is opportune time for a good hard look into the kind of future you may reasonably expect. Let's take a look into your future. No crystal ball needed. Observation, study and experience all furnish fairly dependable premises for propitious predictions.

Now You're President

You've reached the top of your organization. You're now head man in your company. You've achieved your goal of a corporation presidency. Now you can breathe a deep sigh of relief and settle down to enjoy the fruits of your labor ... so you think.

Don't be fooled!

Nothing could be farther from truth. Fact is, the next year or two will no doubt be the most uncomfortable of your entire career. Ask any corporation president who's "been there"; he'll set you straight on how easy it isn't.

After your first couple of years in the president's chair, things should ease up for you a bit . . . other things being equal. But don't regard the president's job as such a snap that you can entirely relax. That's when a lot of up-and-coming vice presidents step up — when the president starts taking it too easy.

At First, You're On Trial

When your board of directors names you president, you'll be ready. But let's take a little more time right now, looking ahead to that day . . . so you'll be all the way ready to serve as your firm's chief executive officer.

Your first reaction will be *elation* . . . generouly seasoned with becomingly modest pride. After all (you'll be thinking on that day), haven't you been planning and working toward this day ever since you made up your mind to become head of the firm before forty?

Everyone is heaping congratulations upon congratulations. Chances are you'll be honored with a dinner, or at least a luncheon with something better than the 85¢ Business Man's Blue Plate. Toasts will be offered. (You'll get the roasting later.) Everyone will express confidence in you, and in the future of the company. Perhaps you may even find a few people who previously took you only half seriously, now making a big play for your attention and approval. It's not improbable that a few of your long-lost friends, down on their luck or looking for better jobs, will get in touch with you.

"It's a great life," you may be tempted to think. "Now I'm going to really enjoy life."

Then you'll preside at your first big executive meeting. At first you'll be a little nervous, no doubt; but that won't be half as bad as feeling that everyone is watching intently to see how you perform as top man in an important commercial enterprise. That's when you'll wake up to the fact that you are still on trial . . . and, to a large degree, you'll remain on trial until the day you say "I retire."

You're The "Man Of Decisions"

Surely, you'll say, "this is no time for relaxing." Maybe you've become. pretty good at golf or poker or even butterflying in the upper social strata. Now, chances are, you'll be spending fewer evenings with the boys — or girls, as the case may be.

Not only will you feel a strong sense of responsibility to the hundreds or perhaps thousands of employees dependent on you for a measure of security, and the stockholders who expect a return on their investment . . . you'll also realize that being president is an entirely different kind of job from any you've had before.

Suddenly you'll be the Man Of Decisions. You'll be expected to make decisions on matters that may be foreign to you . . . or, at least, where you do not have thorough technical knowledge. This, in spite of your years with the company, and all the time you'll have put in trying to learn all phases of the business. (That's when you'll breathe a silent prayer of thanks for a staff that can advise you and keep you on the beam.)

Without a doubt, you'll be astounded at the number of problems that come up from day to day. You'll be tempted to think everything is suddenly going to pot. These pesky problems just started popping out since you took over, you'll start thinking.

But don't think down that road. Don't be discouraged. Those problems were there before you. Some of them, maybe, were waiting just for you . . . and they may be a part of the reason you were named president.

Of course, you didn't hear about all these problems until you got there, in the president's chair. You were so active in other areas of your firm's operation that you didn't look for these problems, and they didn't present themselves where you were. Now, you're completely and finally responsible for everything that happens. You're the one who must look those problems squarely in the face . . . and make the decisions.

A warehouseman falls and breaks his arm. Unless your firm is a really big outfit, you'll be directly concerned with that problem. Somebody else will take him to the hospital, of course; but before the record is closed you'll have to make a decision or two — about workmen's compensation, a loan to the injured man to keep up his swimming pool payments, correcting the hazard that caused his fall, or some other detail connected with the accident. No matter how much authority you've delegated, you'll have to make a decision or two before that matter is finally settled.

Maybe the problem is merely a drop in profit this month from a year ago — *merely* a drop? A very slight drop can sometimes start questions circulating about you! The janitor isn't likely to do much worrying about that slight drop in profits, so long as he gets his check on Friday. But what of your directors — and those inquisitive stockholders, bless 'em? They're *your* bosses, remember. That matter of monthly profit is something you'll be working on, and probably worrying about, into the wee small hours now and then.

Don't Give Problems Time To Grow

Yes, a smooth-running organization, and one that is continuously expanding in size and profit, is your direct concern . . .night and day, and Sunday too.

If you're smart, you'll learn to take these grave responsibilities in stride. You'll develop a sense of proportion that will keep you from worrying about things that can be improved only by action, not by fretting. You'll find ways to get your mind off business occasionally . . . some form of ulcer-insurance to help you rebuild your strength for the next gruelling task.

But, any way you look at it, the day you achieve your goal of a corporation presidency you become a new person. In some ways, you'll be a lonely person, because there will be many things on your mind which cannot be confided to your best friend . . . not even to your wife.

Above all, you'll feel a tremendous challenge . . . a challenge all the more meaningful because you now have an organization and resources behind you that will, if used properly, permit you to make the most of your opportunities. You'll wish there were more hours in every day, more days in every week. There'll be so much to be done, and you the sparkplug to get them started . . . and you'll need the kind of "hot tip" your auto mechanic talks about (not the kind you pick up at the race track).

Experience Will Bring Confidence

At first, no doubt, you'll harbor questions about your capacity to comprehend and weld together all the divergent factions within your organization. But don't worry. Experience will bring confidence. Not only will you develop confidence in yourself, but you'll share a mutual confidence with your top executive staff.

Each of these executives will be different. That's good. One will think conservatively; another, almost radically. Another will demonstrate decisiveness, while still another will prefer to withhold judgment until he confers with members of his own department. The very fact that your executives are different, and think differently, makes them of inestimable value to you in managing the company. With built-in checks and balances, there is less chance of going out beyond the continental shelf where the deep waters of poor decisions can swallow you up in failure.

Then, one day you'll discover that your staff is no longer watching for little signs of weakness in your leadership. They will give their loyalty and confidence in the only way they are worth anything . . . voluntarily. Your staff will recognize you as their leader and, while they may not agree with everything you say or do, they will be behind you all the way.

Surprisingly, the biggest evidence you'll have that your staff members accept you as boss is when they start arguing freely whenever they think your viewpoint should be changed. "Beware the yes-man," it has been aptly said: "he'll also say 'yes' to your doom." Consider yourself lucky if you have an executive staff that thinks enough of you to resist your actions when they think you are wrong. Such subordinates will help you keep out of trouble.

INITIATIVE And TEAMWORK . . .
Your Job Is To Supply Enough For The Whole Company

Now that you've reached the top, you'll need to emphasize your strongest leadership qualities.

Run back through the chapter headings of this book. They'll serve as a check list of the many qualities you'll need to run your company successfully. If you've been developing these qualities over the years, you'll have a head start toward administering your company in a creditable manner.

On your way up you excelled in your specialty . . . accounting, research, production, sales, or whatever. Now, as president, you'll have many jobs and you must excell in all of them. You will have to decide fiscal questions that are too big for your chief accountant. You'll have to find answers that your sales manager cannot come up with, good as he may be. Often, you must be better than your best executives, in their own special areas — but without squelching their initiative.

Of course, the office of president carries weight of itself. Sometimes you'll be able to do a better selling job than your sales manager, not because you're a better salesman but because you're president. Being president, you're in a position to be a "super salesman (the man from home office, with special prices)." You'll have to play that role from time to time, no doubt; but when you do, don't squelch the initiative of the executive you're helping.

This suggests two fundamentals so important that they can make or break you as head of your firm. These fundamentals:

(1) *Initiative;*
(2) *Teamwork.*

Note the order. That's important, too.

The only purpose in having a president for your firm is to make the company move forward. No company moves forward very impressively unless and until all members of the team are working together harmoniously.

All this starts with *initiative.*

A good president *makes* things happen. He doesn't sit down and await developments. A study of result-getters at the head of outstanding corporations shows that five basic qualities set them apart from other managers and adminstrators:

1. They have an *inner drive* that less effective managers lack.
2. They know how to sort out the *vital* from the *trivial.*
3. They know how to *tap and use* the *ideas of others.*
4. They are *tough-minded.*
5. They take *obstacles in stride.*

As head of your company, you'll need all these traits if you are to successfully cope with the large size of your organization and the wide range of problems you'll meet.

And they all add up to *initiative* . . . that salient inner quality that helps plowboys become presidents.

You Provide The Spark

True, you'll have men (and women) on your team with tremendous amounts of innate initiative. You should encourage and even stimulate this initiative. But these subordinate executives cannot provide the kind of initiative needed to make your firm move forward *in toto.* Such initiative must come from the top. It's your job to view the over-all picture and provide the spark to make your company progress steadily.

This is not to say that all the good ideas will be yours. Far from it. That's why you'll have to encourage and tap the ideas of others all down the line.

Encouraging and tapping the ideas of others in your firm may not come naturally to you. It does not come naturally to every man.

When you become president, it will be very easy to get so busy that you overlook the importance of this sort of relationship with subordinates.

An apropos incident is recorded about William M. Jeffers, dynamic President of Union Pacific Railroad, who came up from the ranks as so many railroad heads have done. This significant incident, early during his presidency, directed 'Big Bill' Jeffers' attention to the paramount importance of the human quality in business:

A locomotive engineer who had known President Jeffers "down the line" in earlier years came with an idea about some mechanical problem. Jeffers answered casually and a bit thoughtlessly, being concerned at that moment with some administrative problem which he considered much more important. The engineer thought the idea deserved more attention. He moved toward the door with this remark: "Bill, don't ever get so damned busy that you haven't time to think." Jeffers immediately called the man back, thanked him for opening his eyes to the importance of taking time to encourage ideas and to listen to any and every member of the team. Soon it was a policy up and down the UP line that no executive could be too busy to open his door to any employee with criticism or suggestions.

You may not be a railroader, but I daresay your company can use that Union Pacific "open door" system with the same sort of happy results. There's no better way to foster teamwork . . . no more effective way to multiply your own initiative.

Of course, you can't be expected to waste your time on matters of secondary importance. You just won't have that much time. You'll be obliged to delegate most details to others. You'll be forced to separate the vital from the trivial.

You'll have to be tough-minded with subordinates who block progress . . . but only after making every effort to persuade by reason. (How and why subordinates block progress will usually reveal themselves to you as individual problems, which you'll quickly recognize and quickly dispose of, if you're as good as executive as you should be. These problems are like low hurdles . . . hurdles you'll leap over every day, in stride.)

If obstacles floor you, then you'd better not try to run the firm. If problems frighten you, you're not presidential timber. You must learn to take obstacles in your stride, and clear them easily, like the champion hurdler. This calls for a philosophical attitude, and other characteristics you'll have ample opportunity to develop as years add to your experience with people.

About that *philosophical attitude*: that's another one of the premiums you'll be paying on your ulcer insurance. Keep those premiums paid.

Initiative Only The Start

What will make it possible for you to come through with flying colors on all these points? It's *drive* . . . the kind of drive that will not be held back . . an inner restlessness to get on with the job.

But *initiative* is only the start of the process. An abundance of initiative will not get you far if you don't know how to encourage people to work together harmoniously.

Teamwork is indispensible to a progressing organization. See to good teamwork and your firm will prosper.

As president, you'll have to be the cohesive force that brings opposing personalities together in a well-disciplined and enthusiastic body . . . ready, willing, and eager to give you the support needed to move forward.

The preceding chapters of this book have been designed to help you develop into the kind of person who stimulates teamwork. If you've studied them, and after you've applied the principles and thoughts set forth, then you'll be ready for this challenge . . . and this challenge (to achieve a high degree of teamwork in your firm) will probably be the biggest of your entire career.

Teamwork — THE Essential

Teamwork is so important in directing from the top that some managers often give in to questionable opinions from subordinates, just to preserve harmony. That's why I believe so strongly in group meetings to decide important policy matters. Group meetings mean better decisions. Every executive concerned has a part in making the policy; thus, they are more eager to carry out the policy in a spirit of teamwork.

I know of one successful corporation president (he ran a $4,000,000 company before he was 25) who made it a habit to give credit for most ideas to the men who would be primarily responsible for carrying them out. In many instances the ideas were his own, but he managed to plant the seed and to encourage them to grow in the minds of his subordinates — a mark of true leadership. Not infrequently, a good idea so planted and so nourished will come back to you from a person who honestly believes it to be his own.

If this approach sounds strange, just remember that a president gets credit for what is accomplished by the entire organization. Few if any directors will come around to ask whether this or that successful idea was yours. And your stockholders, remember, will be primarily interested in progress and profits. They'll leave the details to you so long as you see they get a good return on their investment.

You Have A Date With Destiny

So now you're president. Congratulations.

You'll have a great deal of fun in your new life as head of your firm. The knowledge that you made it before forty will give you a sense of pride and security that can come only from the confidence of accomplishment.

But, it's not an easy life. You'll work hard . . . and if you stay there, you'll work harder and harder. Pressures will be great, but every once in a while you'll look ahead and realize that even though you have reached your immediate goal, the final objective of your efforts will forever remain in the future.

It's not past achievements that give you your true satisfaction, but tomorrow's potential. That attitude will keep you younger, longer, than most of your contemporaries. That healthy attitude will help you keep out of the Ulcer Club. You'll be working to build something . . . a great career and a great company . . . and you'll enjoy the work immensely.

And, while you may have numerous disappointments along the way, the fun of trying will spur you on to one new undertaking after another. Then you'll know without a doubt that you were destined to become head of your firm before forty.

28

STARTING YOUR OWN BUSINESS
CAN SOMETIMES BRING YOU FASTER SUCCESS

This book deals primarily with climbing the executive ladder within an established business firm. That is the route with which I am more familiar, from personal experience. I believe it is the route by which most of tomorrow's corporation presidents will get there. This chapter on Starting Your Own Business must, therefore, be a bit "second-hand." Take it for what it's worth.

— J.D.H.

There's more than one way to make a big mark in business before you're forty. There's more than one way to become head of your firm. One promising route, though not the easiest nor least risky, is to start your own business.

"But that's so obvious," you say, "it's almost like cheating."

Far from it. This route is paved with more risks than probably any other.

When you start your own business, you start at the top, so to speak . . . and sometimes this can be much, much riskier than starting at the bottom. For one thing, you have that much farther to fall — if you can't stay up there. And, "staying up there" in a business of your own may depend more on factors you cannot control, than will your progress in the slower, surer process of climbing up in an established firm.

True, if your firm clicks, if your product or service catches on quickly, then you're "in." You'll have the great satisfaction that comes only to founders, innovators, pioneers.

Your product or your service may be the best in the world, actu-

177

ally; but if it is not *right for the time,* you'll have a flop on your hands.

Consider the "Henry J," the economical, sturdy small car brought out by Kaiser soon after World War II. In many respects, it was just as good as the small cars (both American and European) which came to popularity ten or twelve years later. The "Henry J" was ahead of its time . . . that's the story of not a few business failures.

Yes, starting your own business is not always without difficulties, not always without heartbreaks. About one business out of four folds up before it's twelve months old. Many firms surviving that first crucial year have plenty tough going the second year, and even the third, or later.

Uncle Sam has recorded business failures for more than half a century. The following table shows average numbers of failures per year in the U. S., since 1900, and the average rate of failure in businesses established one year or more, by decades:

BUSINESS FAILURES IN THE UNITED STATES
1900 — 1949*

YEARS	AVERAGE NO. FAILURES PER YEAR	AVERAGE NO. FAILURES PER 10,000 FIRMS LISTED
1900 to 1909	12,020	90
1910 to 1919	14,530	90
1920 to 1929	20,443	98
1930 to 1939	17,736	86
1940 to 1949	5,910	26
1949 only	9,247	34

You can see that anyone choosing to work his way to the top by starting his own business is treading on risky ground indeed. But, along with the risks, there is great opportunity. Only *you* can decide whether this is the best road for you.

Potential Rewards

What are some of the rewards? How can you minimize the risks? How can you take maximum advantage of opportunities? How can you be sure of having necessary capital? You should seriously consider these and other important questions before you go an inch farther toward setting up your own business.

First . . . about rewards. If your business venture is eminently

*J. K. Lasser, *Business Management Handbook,* 1952 (p. 143).

successful, you will have reached an outstanding position in the business world because you are the one who started it and guided it to greatness. Your position of leadership is both absolute and without challenge. As your company grows and prospers, you will be at the helm, basking in the self-satisfying warmth which only a hard-won victory can bring . . . and enjoying the material benefits of your labors without benefit of ulcers, we'll both hope.

There's another way to make a business of your own pay off in your climb to the top. You can build your firm till it is quite attractive to a larger corporation; then, when you sell your business you can ride into the executive group of the acquiring company.

Samuel Zemurray, President of United Fruit Company, did just that. Born in Russia, he came to America and settled in Selma, Alabama, where he set himself up as a banana jobber. At 33 he started a small importing company to deal primarily in bananas. After some years of friendly though intense competition, his firm was purchased by United Fruit. Within a few years, Zemurray was invited to take over United Fruit's top executive job.

W. Maxey Jarman, Board Chairman of General Shoe Corporation, climbed to the top of his industry by this route. He went with General Shoe when his family's firm, Jarman Shoe Company, was sold to the larger corporation.

This approach can have the additional advantage of paying off very handsomely in dollars. Neison Harris organized The Toni Company (home permanent waves) soon after graduation from Yale. He sold Toni to Gillette for a cool $20,000,000 a few years later. He remained top administrative officer in Toni, while becoming an important executive in the larger Gillette organization.

Whichever of the above-mentioned roads you take, however, it may be well to consider an important trend which appears to be developing in American business. This trend comes from several economic factors that give a decided advantage to large firms.

The direction is definitely toward bigness. A small firm must either become big itself (and fairly quickly), or it must be absorbed by one of the many giant corporations constantly on the lookout for profitable companies to buy.

Why Be Big?

Why is it so important to be big? Some of the reasons are obvious.

More money.

Better facilities for manufacturing and selling.

Talented leadership that increases the probability of success for any new idea or product.

These are the obvious reasons. But there is one great economic factor often overlooked when discussing the advantages of bigness:

Every successful business goes through an almost predictable growth curve. Characteristically, the initial stages are painfully slow. Then business picks up speed as need for the firm's product or service is recognized. During this period, sales increases may be truly astounding. Then comes a leveling off. Often, a firm is hard pressed to keep up with competition. Finally, there's a period of fierce competition, usually accompanied by very small increases in the size of the market for many years running. This is the time when most marginal firms disappear from the scene. In many cases, the entire industry is subjected to small profits, or none.

Secret

The Secret of Successful Bigness is that a large industrial organization is so completely diversified that it may have dozens of products at different stages of this curve, with several others about to be introduced. If one product, or an entire division, gets into trouble because of these economic factors, or because of competition, the effects are considerably less than disastrous on the rest of the organization.

I know of one large national firm that had a huge factory producing an ingredient for the plastics industry. The business operated at a good profit for a dozen years or more. Then its product became obsolete. It just wasn't needed any more. Did this firm shut down and fire its 300-odd workers? No sir! Management simply rolled out a new product from the Research & Development Labs, and put it into production in the very same factory.

This is an advantage large firms have over smaller ones. Often, it is a life-saving advantage. This makes it important that you (in planning to start your own business) plan early to either grow big yourself or merge with a larger corporation. One of the quick ways to grow big is to have an acquisition policy of your own. (While you won't have much money to buy companies at first, you'll do well to plan in that direction.)

That's one way James A. Ryder became, at 38, "No. 2 trucker in the U. S. A." And his nation-wide Ryder System didn't stop growing there; it has even reached Central America.

Ryder started his own business in 1933, with a second-hand truck and plenty of energetic ambition. (He borrowed $300 to buy the truck.) The biggest steps in his corporation's phenomenal growth have been the acquisition of established companies, such as: Great Southern Trucking Company, covering the Southeast out of Jacksonville, Florida; Baker Truck Rental, Denver.

Jim Ryder has built an international transportation enterprise on the foundation of sound build-it-yourself business principles he learned when he had that first truck. Among these principles:

> Serve a well-defined need.
> Save enough from income to always show a profit.
> Surround yourself with specialists.

Now . . . How Do You Get Started?

First, you'll need a good idea. (Unless, of course, you have enough money to buy out an existing business. Which, incidentally, is not a bad idea; it will give you a nucleus from which to build as big and as fast as you can.) But, remember, an idea is not necessarily good because it is original. It will have to be tested. That takes time. It also takes a bit of money, usually. One of the most original-thinking businessmen I know once remarked to me: "If people only knew how many failures I've had for each of my successes . . ."

Test your ideas in a small way before you give up your job or invest any really big money in your venture. Preliminary testing will give you invaluable information on how (or whether) you should proceed. Test to see what kind of market there is for your product or service. Test to find the best, and most economical, way to sell what you have to offer.

Next, you'll need money. Perhaps you've saved a few thousand dollars. You're ready to risk your savings to get your business started. Don't kid yourself, now. For every Jim Ryder or Henry Kaiser, there are perhaps a dozen people who started with the same good ideas . . . but you've never heard of them. They didn't have enough money, or enough understanding creditors . . . or enough of some other necessary ingredient, including (sometimes) "good breaks." But it's fairly certain that those failures didn't have enough money.

Better start out with adequate capital — adequate not only for initial needs, but also a little nest egg for future growth.

How Do You Get Money?

That's a big question . . . sometimes, *the* big question. The answer can be as complicated as the question is big. It's too much to try to answer in detail in this chapter — it would take a book, or more. But, *money can be had.* Here are some possibilities:

Consider investments from people who have nearly as much faith in you as you have in yourself and your idea or product. They may be friends or relatives.

You may have to go out soliciting capital. Your idea may be good enough to warrant a public stock issue at the outset . . . though this is rare for a brand-new company.

At any rate, unless you're pretty well fixed financially, you'll probably have partners at the start . . . maybe silent partners, like most stockholders are, but partners nonetheless. And, your partners will be more interested in profits than in promises. If you can choose partners with a great deal of patience, you'll be that much farther ahead in the long run; they won't be breathing down your neck during the (usually) difficult early period of your business.

Let's go back to that first suggestion: people who have faith in you.

Peter Hurst was 29 when, in 1939, he fled Nazi Germany. His main asset: an idea for a flexible industrial hose with detachable fitting. He landed in Jackson, Michigan, not a big city. He talked about his idea to local businessmen. Soon, ten of them each put up $1,000 to give his idea a trial.

The Aeroquip Corporation was organized in 1940. The first office was one desk, an empty file cabinet, and a drafting board. In 1942, sales were $1,150,000. Military purchases soared as Hurst's idea (which *served* a need at a *saving*) got around. In 1945, sales were $6,000,000; in 1952, $20,000,000.* The ten happiest men in Jackson that year would certainly have included all of those who had invested $1,000 each to get the business started.

Marvin Small, to whom I am indebted for that story on Peter Hurst, points out that,

> with taxes as they stand, you can count on a man or woman in the higher-income brackets being interested in good new products, processes, services . . . At the rates prevailing today, a person in the upper tax brackets would lose only 12¢ to 25¢ on every dollar if a risk investment went *entirely* sour. But if the company should prosper, he could sell his interest and for every dollar of profit add 74¢ net to his capital†

Suggests interesting possibilities, doesn't it? In his most interesting book on financial security, Marvin Small mentions a number

---

*Marvin Small: *How To Attain Financial Security And Self-confidence Without Risking Your Job Or Your Savings* (Simon & Schuster, 1953, p. 263).
†*Ibid.*, p. 265.

of firms in the business of investing in new companies, among them: Rockefeller Brothers, Inc.; J. H. Whitney & Company; American Research & Development Corporation; New Enterprises, Inc.; Burd Brothers; H. E. Talbott Company (the personal risk-venture vehicle of former Secretary of the Air Force Harold Talbott).

Some of the spectacular business successes of the last quarter-century owe their starts to financial aid from such firms; among them: Minute Maid Corporation, McDonnell Aircraft, and Kaman Aircraft Corporation (helicopters).

If you're interested in exploring further down this interesting avenue, you could hardly do better than to get Marvin Small's idea-filled book and then follow up on some of the leads you'll get from it.

Whatever Your Size, Organize

Next, if you're to have something more than a "one-horse business," you'll need an organization. You'll need associates, subordinate executives, team-mates, or whatever you care to call them . . . to help you manage; and you'll have to give them some authority, as discussed in Chapter 15. You will need workers to produce and sell your goods, or services.

Be very careful in selecting your first employees. As your business grows, they will probably take on more and more responsibility. Eventually, they may become key executives in your firm. Be especially careful in selecting them, for nothing could be more disheartening than having to discontinue the services of a long-time associate simply because he could not grow with his job and with the company.

You Grow As You Serve

The DuPont organization tests every new idea or program at an early stage. The test is a simple one: *Does it serve a need?*

If you want to see your company grow over the years, you'll do well to keep asking yourself this same question over and over again: *Does it serve a need?*

In business, you grow only as you serve.

Of course, you and your company will grow faster if you're serving a need which is widely recognized. a need which nearly everybody feels.

Years ago, a lot of mothers felt the need for an extra pair of hands . . .holding baby while twisting a little cotton around a toothpick to clean his ears and nose. Leo Gerstenzang saw the need already felt by mothers . . . and he did something about it: Q-Tips. Dun & Bradstreet soon rated him in the upper bracket.

Most people eat steak, at least once in a while. Most steak that most people eat is a little on the tough, side. Lloyd Rigler and Larry Deutsch, as starving young actors, didn't eat too much steak . . . but they didn't lose their taste for tender T-bone. They went into the dry-cleaning business, and sold mushrooms on the side. Dollars still eluded them, in large numbers. They just couldn't stand those tender, juicy filet mignons at $3.95; so they kept looking till they discovered Adolph's Steak House, where steaks were cheap but *tender*. They became friendly with Adolph. One day he told them of his "secret formula" for tenderizing steaks. They made a deal with him to perfect, package, and market the product — derived mainly from the papaya. In four years, sales went from zero to $500,000 . . . and still climbing.

Marvin Small tells these and other pertinent success stories in his marvelous book on financial security, previously quoted. He concludes that "Adolph's had quietly taken a firm hold on the national market because it filled one of our country's most basic needs — better food at lower prices."

Yes, when you *serve a need at a saving,* you're bound to succeed.

Failure Does Not Preclude Success

It's often said that the mark of a truly great man is found in his *persistence*. Remember how Christopher Morley said it? — "Big shots are little shots who kept on shooting."

A case in point: King C. Gillette's several failures before he struck it rich with the safety razor.

Clarence Saunders had a number of unsuccessful ventures before, and after, his big success with the first self-service grocery store.

Indeed, it is hard to find a really big man who has not, at some time in his life, faced the challenge of a business failure. Disgrace is not in the failure . . . it's in "giving up." It's not *being* down but *staying* down that counts a man out.

Remember, every time you do something wrong you learn a little that should help you on the next try. That's why modern executive training programs stress *doing* by trainees rather than *showing* by trainers. The man on the way up is expected to make some mistakes, as we saw in Chapter 13. But each time you commit an error in judgment on a small problem, you're building up a warehouse full of experience that will help you avoid mistakes on bigger problems sure to come.

The same is true of a business failure. Assuming you are smart enough to avoid making the same mistake twice, you can reasonably expect that your first failure will reduce your chances of failure on the second try.

It Has Been Done . . . Many Times Over

As stated at the head of this chapter, I believe most of tomorrow's leaders of big business will achieve their goals by climbing the executive ladder within established firms. One reason for this belief is the apparent obsession (increasingly evident in our society) with *security,* as distinguished from *opportunity.* The more adventurous, the more self-confident, the more unorthodox will strike out for themselves. They will be the Henry Fords, the Andrew Carnegies, the John D. Rockefellers of the 21st century.

Men of such mind do not so much need the experience and training one gets by starting at the bottom in a well-established firm. Not every such man who starts his own business will make a big mark, of course; but those who do will make marks for others to shoot at for decades to come.

In pursuing such a goal, nothing is more helpful than to read about and study the lives of business leaders who have achieved similar goals. If your inclination and determination are toward starting your own business, I highly recommend your reading whatever you can find about such people. The most convenient place, no doubt, is your public library. In addition to specific listings in the library's card catalog, you will find interesting information about current activities of many business people indexed in such publications as:

> *New York Times* Index
> *Reader's Guide to Periodical Literature*
> *Who's Who in Commerce & Industry*
> Indexes published by some trade publications.

Here are some outstanding people who started their own businesses. The list is by no means complete, with regard to any facet of industry or period of time; it's merely a list of *some* outstanding business founders whose records provide interesting and helpful guideposts.

NOTE: Not all of these people started their businesses *before* forty.

Henry Ford was 40 when he organized Ford Motor Company. Carl Magee was 70 when Magee-Hale Park-O-Meter Company was set up. Persons indicated by asterick (*) had at least some managerial experience in the same industry, before setting up their own firms. Note that most of these leaders started themselves in business without such experience.

REMMIE L. ARNOLD	Arnold Pen Co. — Second largest in world
JOHN JACOB ASTOR	Fur trader; real estate
OLE BARDAHL	Bardahl Mfg. Company — oil
STEPHEN D. BECHTEL	Bechtel Corporation — construction
VINCENT BENDIX	Bendix Aviation; also automobiles, appliances
CLARENCE BIRDSEYE	Birdseye Frozen Foods
WALTER H. BOWES	Pitney-Bowes — postage machines
WALTER E. BOTTHOF	Standard Rate & Data Service
S. F. BRIGGS	Briggs & Stratton — motors
ALAN BRITE	*Copper Brite* Cleaner
LENA (LANE) BRYANT	women's clothing
GEORGE A. BUNTING	Noxema — medicated cream
ANDREW CARNEGIE*	steel
WALTER P. CHRYSLER*	Chrysler Motor Company
WILLIAM H. DANFORTH	Ralston-Purina Company — cereals, feed
ROBERT DeGRAFF*	Pocket Books, Inc.
JAMES D. DOLE	Hawaiian Pineapple Company
ROBERT DOLLAR	Dollar Steamship Lines
ELMER DOOLIN	Fritos — corn snacks
DONALD W. DOUGLAS*	Douglas Aircraft Company
JAMES B. DUKE	tobacco (He was rated America's No. 3 philanthropist when he established The Duke Endowment and Duke University.)
GEORGE EASTMAN	Eastman Kodak Company
OLE EVINRUDE	Evinrude (outboard) Motors
WILLIAM GEORGE FARGO*	American Express Co.; Wells-Fargo Express
MARSHALL FIELD*	merchandising
HARVEY S. FIRESTONE*	Firestone Tire & Rubber Company
HENRY FORD	Ford Motor Company
AUGUST FRUEHAUF	Fruehauf Trailer Company
ALFRED E. FULLER	Fuller Brushes
J. PAUL GETTY	oil
A. P. GIANNINI	Bank of America
KING C. GILLETTE	Gillette Safety Razor Company
SAMUEL GOLDWYN	motion pictures
GUGGENHEIM BROTHERS	mining, smelting
C. WILSON HARDER*	National Federation of Independent Business (largest membership of any business association in U. S.)
NEISON HARRIS	Toni Home Permanent
WILLIAM RANDOLPH HEARST	Hearst Newspapers

MILTON HERSHEY	Hershey Chocolate Company
H. J. HEINZ	H. J. Heinz Company — food
ANDREW J. HIGGINS	Higgins Industries; others — lumber, boats
CONRAD HILTON	hotels around the world
HARVEY HUBBELL	Harvey Hubbell, Inc. — electrical equip't
HOWARD JOHNSON	restaurants
JESSE JONES*	lumber, finance, publishing; Secretary of Commerce under F. D. Roosevelt
BILL and FAIE JOYCE	Joyce Casuals — shoes
HENRY J. KAISER	construction, metals, autos, other
S. S. KRESGE	merchandising — some 700 stores in U. S. and Canada
R. G. LETOURNEAU	heavy machinery
ALEX LEWYT	vacuum cleaners
EDWIN ALBERT LINK	Link Aviation, Inc. — flight trainer
HENRY R. LUCE	*Time-Life-Fortune*
CARL MAGEE	Magee-Hale Park-O-Meter Company
GLENN L. MARTIN	aircraft
GEORGE L. MCCARTHY	Recordak
EUGENE F. MCDONALD, JR.*	Zenith Radio & Television
CHARLES E. MERRILL	Merrill Lynch, Pierce, Fenner & Smith
JOHN PIERPONT MORGAN*	J. P. Morgan & Company — banking
ARTHUR J. MORRIS*	"Morris Plan" system of banking
A. C. NIELSEN	A. C. Nielsen Company — world's largest marketing research company
JOHN H. PATTERSON	National Cash Register Company
EDWIN W. PAULEY	oil, real estate, construction, public service; served under President Truman with rank of Ambassador
J. C. PENNEY	J. C. Penney Company — some 1,700 stores
HERMAN PERL	head of 18 corporations, emphasizing salesmanship
LYDIA E. PINKHAM	patent medicine
ARTHUR H. PITNEY	Pitney-Bowes — postage meters
ABE PLOUGH	Plough, Inc. — pharmaceuticals
JAMES H. RAND	Remington-Rand — office equipment
FREDERICK B. RENTSCHLER	Wright Aeronautical Corporation; Pratt & Whitney; United Aircraft
R. J. REYNOLDS	tobacco
RICHARD S. REYNOLDS, JR.	Reynolds Metals; Reynolds & Company (banking)
CHARLES H. REVSON	Revlon — cosmetics
RICHARD S. RHEEM	Rheem Mfg. Company — water heaters
WILLIAM ROSENBERG	Industrial Luncheon Service
JOHN D. ROCKEFELLER	Standard Oil Company
HENRY ROSENFELD*	Henry Rosenfeld, Inc. — clothing
HELENA RUBINSTEIN	cosmetics
MARGARET RUDKIN	Pepperidge Farm Bread
JAMES A. RYDER	Ryder System, Inc. — truck transport
CLARENCE SAUNDERS	Piggly-Wiggly — self-service grocery
HAROLD SCHAFER	Glass Wax

ROBERT SCHNEIDER	Diners' Club
ISAAC M. SINGER	Singer Sewing Machine Company
ROSS DAVID SIRAGUSA	Admiral Radio, TV & Appliances
GUSTAVUS F. SWIFT	Swift & Company — meat
JUAN T. TRIPPE	Pan American World Airways
CORNELIUS VANDERBILT	sea and rail transportation
JOHN WANAMAKER	merchandising
GEORGE WESTINGHOUSE	railway and electrical equipment
ARTHUR A. WILLARD	storage batteries
F. W. WOOLWORTH	merchandising
JOHN A. ZEHNTBAUER	Jantzen Knitting Mills

Some incidental information about a few of those leaders:

... Some — like J. P. Morgan and Richard S. Reynolds, Jr. — were born to wealth; but they didn't let money stand in their way. They agreed with Henry Ford's idea that "you either *use* or *lose* money."

... Many women business leaders — including Lena (Lane) Bryant and Lydia E. Pinkham — have embarked on business careers when they found themselves impecunious widows. Necessity was the mother of their inventive and imaginative enterprise.

... Several, like Ole Bardahl (Norway) and Helena Rubinstein (Poland), came to a strange country to begin their business careers; and had language and social barriers to overcome, in addition to more usual hazards.

... Among those (*) who had considerable experience in their chosen field before setting up their own business is Robert De-Graff. He had risen to a position of considerable authority and prestige with Doubleday & Company, one of the leading publishers, when he decided to try the idea of Pocket Books — paper-bound reprints of well-known books. He sold the idea to another publisher, Simon & Schuster, who helped set up the new corporation. DeGraff was Chairman of the Board from the beginning. In fourteen years he accumulated a tidy sum from Pocket Books, and retired in 1952 — age: (You'll find his story in Marvin Small's *How To Attain Financial Security*, and in the *New York Herald-Tribune* of October 19, 1952.)

... John H. Patterson's dedication to *singleness of purpose* enabled him to exert his very constructive influence on a number of subordinates who subsequently guided other firms; among these eminent businessmen: Thomas J. Watson, of IBM.

... Patience is a very necessary virtue, sometimes. It took Arthur

Pitney nearly twenty years to get his postage meter accepted by the Post Office Department in Washington.

... Zenith's Gene McDonald had been successful in business since, at 20; he organized an auto finance company. Among other enterprises: used cars and a body manufacturing firm. Then came radio. He foresaw the popularity of this new industry and hitched his new wagon to that star. The famous Zenith Hearing Aid resulted from his own personal need; an auto accident at the height of his career cost him hearing in one ear.

... Jesse Jones (Secretary of Commerce), Edwin W. Pauley (World War II Reparations Commission) and John Wanamaker (Postmaster General) became sufficiently independent, financially, that they could afford to serve in high government posts in the prime of life.

In Conclusion

There's a great deal to be said for becoming head of the firm by starting your own business. If you are willing to accept the difficulties and hazards, and possible heartbreak, of early struggling against tremendous odds . . . then go to it. If you are willing to back your ideas with your last penny, you might make it. If you're willing to work at least twice as hard as you would for anyone else, then you have one of the essentials to success. And, if you are willing to face the possibility (nay, perhaps the probability) of failure (at least on your first try) , then you'll do well to consider this as one of the more promising routes to the top of a corporation of importance before you're forty.

Key for Scoring APTITUDE QUESTIONS, Pages 10, 11 and 12.

15 or fewer questions answered "Yes"	LIMITED APTITUDE
20 or more questions answered "Yes"	FAIR APTITUDE
25 or more questions answered "Yes"	GOOD APTITUDE
28 or more questions answered "Yes"	EXCELLENT APTITUDE

SCORING ON MAJOR SUCCESS FACTORS

(For explanation, see Chapter 1, page 8.)

		SCORE
1.	Hard work	100
2.	Tackling tough problems	97
3.	Happy marriage and moral support	93
4.	Opportunism	90
5.	Singleness of purpose	87
6.	Smooth personal relationships	85
7.	Delegating responsibility	80
8.	Complete knowledge of firm's operation	79
9.	Ability to make decisions	77
10.	Planned public relations	77
11.	Participating in civic affairs	67
12.	Luck	66
13.	Being an expert in something	65
14.	Trade association activity	57
15.	Socializing with customers	55
16.	Monetary incentive	52
17.	Enthusiasm for the job and ability to inspire associates	50
18.	Putting up a front	46
19.	Company politics	46
20.	Detailed career planning	40
21.	Socializing with co-workers	30
22.	Desire to learn	24
23.	Creative thinking	13

A SELECT BIBLIOGRAPHY

A. Books

This list does not include all volumes consulted in preparation of this book. It is a select list of recent and not-too-ancient books which should be interesting to the young executive on his way to the top, and to the student who looks toward a career in commerce.

Black, James Menzies. *How To Grow In Management.* Englewood Cliffs, New Jersey: Prentice-Hall, 1957.
> Helpful "Pink Sheet" summaries and self-evaluation check lists at end of each chapter. Highly recommended for sustained study.

Brophy, Loire. *There's Plenty Of Room At The Top.* New York: Simon & Schuster, 1946.

Carnegie, Dale. *How To Win Friends And Influence People.* New York: Simon & Schuster, 1936.
> One of the best. More than 50 printings in Pocket Book editions alone.

Cerami, Charles A. *Successful Leadership In Business.* New York: Prentice-Hall, Inc., 1955.
> A step-by-step program for increasing your value to your firm.

DeArmond, Fred. *The Executive At Work.* Englewood Cliffs, New Jersey: Prentice-Hall, 1958.
> Fast-paced. Easy reading. Many interesting examples.

Forbes, B. C. (Ed.) *America's 50 Foremost Business Leaders.* New York: B. C. Forbes & Sons Publishing Company, 1948.

Forbes, B. C. (Ed.) 101 *Unusual Experiences.* New York: B. C. Forbes & Sons, 1952.

Frailey, L. E. *This Way Up.* Chicago: American Technical Society, 1946.

Gates and Miller. *Personal Adjustment To Business.* New York: Prentice-Hall, 1958.

Hill, Napoleon. *How To Raise Your Own Salary.* Chicago: Napoleon Hill Associates, Div. of W. Clement Stone Enterprises.

Kahn, Harold S. *You Can Be Successful And Follow The Golden Rule.* New York: Wilcox & Follett Company.

Keyes, Kenneth, Jr. *How To Develop Your Thinking Ability.* New York: McGraw-Hill, 1950.
A most helpful book for anybody who will use it.

Kienzle, George J. and Edward H. Dare. *Climbing The Executive Ladder.* New York: McGraw-Hill, 1950.
Especially helpful helf-rating scales, and a most interesting chapter on "How to Relax."

Kleiser, Grenville. *Training For Power And Leadership.* Garden City, New York: Garden City Publishing Company, 1923.

Laird, Drs. Donald A. and Eleanor C. *Practical Business Psychology.* New York: McGraw-Hill, 1956.

Marquis, A. N., Co. (Pub.) *Who's Who In Commerce & Industry.* Chicago: Marquis-Who's Who. Various editions since 1936.

Mead, Shepherd. *How To Succeed In Business Without Really Trying.* New York: Simon & Schuster, 1952.
Sound advice wrapped up in easy reading, with cartoons.

Panzer, Martin. *Raise Your Sights.* New York: Prentice-Hall 1947.

Prevette, Earl. *How To Turn Your Ability Into Cash.* New York: Prentice-Hall, 1953.

Reilly, William J. *Successful Human Relations.* New York: Harper & Bros., 1952.

Simmons, Harry. *Business Success Handbook.* New York: Harper & Bros., 1956.

Simon & Schuster (Pub.) 100 *Stories Of Business Success.* From articles in *Fortune* Magazine. New York: Simon & Schuster, 1954.

Small, Marvin. *How To Attain Financial Security And Self-Confidence Without Risking Your Job Or Your Savings* New York: Simon & Schuster, 1953.

Jam-packed with brief stories of successful businessmen, and women. Many concrete, down-to-earth suggestions for getting your own business underway. A good book to have on your night table, or by your easy chair.

Starch, Daniel. *How To Develop Your Executive Ability.* New York: Harper & Bros., 1943.

Taylor, C. W., Jr. (Pub) *Eminent Americans,* 1954 and 1957 eds. Published at Palo Alto, California.

B. Magazines

In addition to the leading trade publications in your field, you should be acquainted with the following magazines which address themselves to practically all phases of business:

Barron's
Business Week
Dun's Review & Modern Industry
Forbes
Fortune
Journal of Commerce
Nation's Business
U. S. News & World Report
Wall Street Journal

John D. Horn became head of his firm, House of Huston, Inc., at the age of 32. When the company was sold to Sterling Drug, Inc., he remained as President of that subsidiary for an additional two years, until he decided to devote his full time to the acquisition and building of several other corporations. Today he is President and majority stockholder of two candy firms, a consulting company and director of five firms ranging from construction to consumer products. Sales of these corporations, in which Mr. Horn is an important stockholder, exceed $20,000,000.00.

Mr. Horn's rapid rise in business has been in the American tradition of firm purpose, continual study and hard work. He was partner in a small printing firm during his college years; he did graduate work at Columbia University while employed in the Market Research Department of Colgate-Palmolive Co. At 25 he became Vice President of House of Huston, one of the country's leading manufacturers and distributors of pet care items — where he helped build sales from $80,000.00 to more than $4,000,000.00 in six years.

In the course of his busy career Mr. Horn has also managed to acquire a pretty wife and six children—the first five of whom were boys.

NOTES

NOTES

NOTES

NOTES

NOTES

NOTES

NOTES

NOTES

NOTES